Inheriting An

JACQUELINE VAN MAARSEN was born in 1929 in Amsterdam, where she still lives. Since 1986 she has been lecturing on Anne Frank, and on discrimination, in schools all over the world. She is the author of *My Name is Anne, She Said, Anne Frank: The Memoirs of Anne Frank's Best Friend*.

BRIAN DOYLE has translated a wide variety of academic works from Dutch/Flemish into English and since training and registration with the Flemish Literature Fund (VFL)/Dutch Foundation for the Production and Translation of Dutch Literature (NLPVF), he has been involved in the translation of literary fiction and non-fiction. Recent projects include Cynthia Mc Leod's *The Free Negress Elisabeth* (Arcadia, 2008) and Jef Geeraerts' *The PG* (Bitter Lemon Press, 2009). His translations of Pieter Waterdrinker's *The German Wedding* (Atlantic Grove) and Christiaan Wiejts' *The Window Dresser* (Arbeiderspers) are scheduled for publication in November 2009.

Inheriting Anne Frank

JACQUELINE VAN MAARSEN

Translated from the Dutch by Brian Doyle

ARCADIA BOOKS

Arcadia Books Ltd
15–16 Nassau Street
London W1W 7AB

www.arcadiabooks.com

First published in the United Kingdom 2009
Originally published under the title *De Erflaters* by Uitgeverij Cossee, Amsterdam 2004
Copyright © Jacqueline van Maarsen 2004
This English translation from the Dutch © Brian Doyle 2009

Jacqueline van Maarsen has asserted her moral right to be identified as the author of this work in accordance with the Copyright, Designs and Patents Act, 1988.

All rights reserved. No part of this publication may be reproduced in any form or by any means without the written permission of the publishers.

A catalogue record for this book is available from the British Library.

ISBN 978-1-906413-27-9

Typeset in Minion by MacGuru Ltd
Printed in Finland by WS Bookwell

This book was published with the support of the Foundation for the Production and Translation of Dutch Literature.

Arcadia Books supports PEN, the fellowship of writers who work together to promote literature and its understanding. English PEN upholds writers' freedoms in Britain and around the world, challenging political and cultural limits on free expression. To find out more, visit www.englishpen.org or contact
English PEN, 6–8 Amwell Street, London EC1R 1UQ

Arcadia Books distributors are as follows:

in the UK and elsewhere in Europe:
Turnaround Publishers Services
Unit 3, Olympia Trading Estate
Coburg Road
London N22 6TZ

in the US and Canada:
Independent Publishers Group
814 N. Franklin Street
Chicago, IL 60610

in Australia:
Tower Books
PO Box 213
Brookvale, NSW 2100

Suffolk County Council	
07470159	
Askews	Dec-2009
940.5318	£11.99

Arcadia

Contents

PART ONE
A Response / 1

PART TWO
Trouble in Paris / 67

PART THREE
Remember Every Last Detail / 99

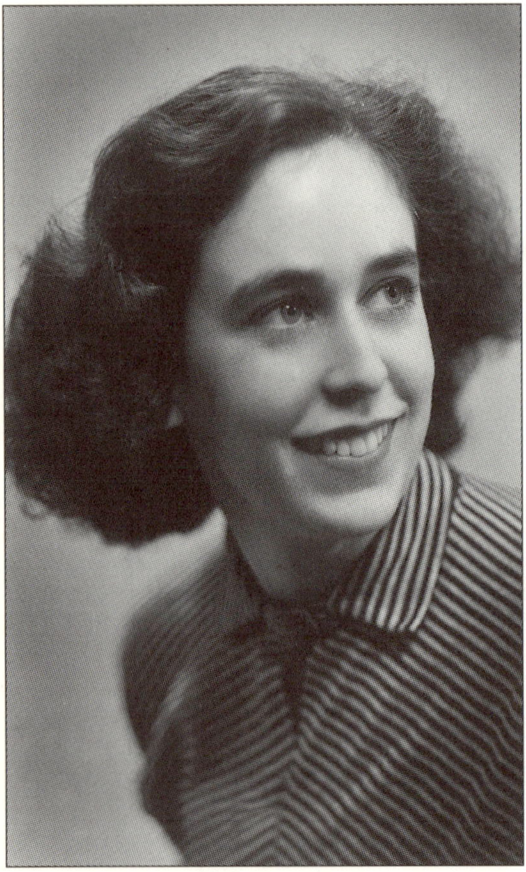

... for the girl who can write no longer

PART ONE

A RESPONSE

I

I'm gazing out of the window at the river flowing past my hotel in Basel. The Rhine's currents are powerful at this time of the year, making upstream traffic a slow process. Ships heading downstream, on the other hand, are able to cut through the waters at a rate of knots.

It was 1970 and the last day of our vacation. We had spent the afternoon with Otto Frank and were planning to return to Amsterdam the next morning after a quick visit to the paper museum. My mother and my sister had been looking after the children for a week.

Anne's father had come to Amsterdam the previous spring and brought me a copy of *Weerklank – Response*, a collection of reactions penned by admirers of Anne's writings that had just been published. After reading the book, I realised just how much it must have consoled Otto to have received so many letters from people all over the world who had read *The Diary of a Young Girl*. Otto told me that he answered all of them. It wasn't so much Anne's fate that inspired people, but the ideas and ideals her diary aroused in those who read it. After all, there was little to know about the months following the betrayal and arrest that ultimately led to her death in March 1945. A short note at the end of the diary makes only a brief mention of the place and circumstances surrounding the death of seven of the eight inhabitants of the *Achterhuis*, the annexe behind Otto Frank's office building in Amsterdam.

I had been able to ask him questions for the first time

that afternoon. I had never inquired about his interests and preoccupations in the past, not even in relation to the Anne Frank Foundation. He probably thought I wasn't interested, but in truth the idea of asking questions about the things I had read in the newspapers pained me, and I was certain he must have found them far from pleasant. They dealt for the most part with political matters and problems relating to the board of the Foundation and the way it was being run. Our discussion that summer day in Basel was reason enough for him to fetch Anne's original diary from the safe.

I now held Anne's unassuming tartan-covered diary in my hands for the first time and was able to read the letters she had addressed to me. First the letter she had copied into her diary in September 1942. 'I hope we remain "best friends" until we meet again'; and then the second letter with the words 'I think about you so often.' I knew the letters off by heart – her father had sent me copies twenty-five years earlier – but this was the first opportunity I had had to read them in her own handwriting.

This is the promised farewell letter

25 September 1942

Dear Jacqueline,
I'm writing this letter to say goodbye, this will probably come as something of a surprise, but fate will have it no other way, I have to go (as you'll probably have heard) with my family, I'm sure you know why.
    When you called on Sunday afternoon I couldn't say anything, my mother wouldn't let me, the whole house was upside down and the front door was locked. Hello was supposed to

make an appearance, but no one opened the door. I can't write to everyone so that's why I'm writing to you alone. I assume you won't speak with anyone about this letter or mention who sent it. If you would be generous enough to correspond with me in secret I would really appreciate it. <u>Ask Mrs Gies!!!</u> I hope we'll see each other again soon, but it probably won't be before the end of the war. If Lies* or anyone else ever asks whether you've heard from me, don't say yes whatever you do, it would put Mrs Gies and the rest of us in mortal danger and I hope I can rely on your discretion. You can tell people later, of course, that you received one letter from me, a farewell letter. All the best to you, Jackie, I'll be looking out for a sign of life from you, hope to see you again soon.

Your '<u>best</u>' friend <u>Anne</u>

P.S. I hope we'll remain '<u>best</u> friends' until we meet again <u>Bye-bye</u>

<u>Second Letter</u>

25 September 1942

Dear Jackie,
Your letter really cheered me up, if none of the Germans have been to our house, feel free to go to Mr Goldschmith and pick up some books, notebooks and games, you can keep them or look after them for me or give them to Mrs Gies. I forgot to mention last time I wrote that you <u>mustn't</u> keep my letters because <u>no one</u> must ever find them. So cut them into tiny pieces, as we did that time on the roof with those instructions from Mother's box. I hope you'll do it. How is everyone, I can't

---

* Hannah, known to her friends as Lies (J.v.M)

write anything about myself, of course. I think about you so often. How's Ilse doing, is she still around. Mrs Gies told me that Lies is still here. Beyond the fact that we have company and we're not bored, there's nothing more I'm allowed to write about our life, it might be scary but it's interesting for later. I have to keep it short, see you, with a little kiss from
    Anne

Otto sat opposite me in silence, staring at my face as I read. As always, I tried to hide my feelings from him, but it wasn't long before they got the better of me and I handed back the book with a red face and tears in my eyes. I was also moved by the fact that she had invented my response to her first letter, a response I couldn't have written because she hadn't been allowed to send her farewell letter. Otto once mentioned that Anne had wanted to ask Miep to pass her letter on to me – Miep lived opposite us on Hunzestraat – but had understood after a bout of squabbling that it could have been dangerous. No one, including myself, was allowed to know the family's whereabouts. I presumed that the Frank family had fled to Switzerland and that was it. Everyone who knew the family thought the same. As evidence, Otto had deliberately left a scrap of paper behind in the empty house with an address in Switzerland.

    It struck me all at once how much Otto and Anne resembled one another, not only physically, but also in terms of character. I hadn't thought much about it during his many visits just after the war, when he wanted me to tell him all about my friendship with Anne. I had to force myself in those days not to be too distant, which was something I couldn't help, something Anne had also found difficult to understand at first. I had grown up since then and was more approachable, but his extrovert personality still bothered me now and again.

Otto Frank stayed with Miep Gies and her husband for a couple of years after the war but no longer felt at home in Amsterdam. Miep and Jan Gies had lived opposite us on Hunzestraat in Amsterdam's River District during the war and later moved to another house further along the same street. Miep had helped attend to the needs of the eight people who had gone into hiding in the *Achterhuis*, providing them with food and other necessities in the utmost secrecy.

Otto Frank married Elfriede Geiringer in 1954 and moved to Basel where his mother, brother and sister lived. They met each other for the first time in Odessa when Otto was on his way to the Netherlands after being liberated from Auschwitz by the Russians in January 1945. Fritzi – as she was known – and her daughter Eva had arrived in Odessa from the concentration camp at around the same time. They met again in Amsterdam some time later while examining the lists posted by the Red Cross of those who had died in the camps. The lists were based on detailed information kept by the Nazis themselves and indicated exact places and dates. Otto found his wife Edith's name on such a list, although he had already heard that she had passed away in Auschwitz. Fritzi also discovered the names of her deceased husband and son on the lists and Otto the names of his two daughters Margot and Anne. By that time he had already been told about their deaths by two sisters who lived in Rotterdam. They had both been present when first Margot and then Anne succumbed to typhoid in Bergen-Belsen.

In the years after the war I did my best to put the past

behind me. I never spoke about my wartime tribulations or my deceased family and friends. Anne and my youngest cousins Deetje and Meta were closest to me and I tried to think about the dreadful fate they had undergone as little as possible. I learned from the information on the lists that Deetje and Meta had been gassed together with their entire family immediately after arrival at Sobibor. Anne's father told me what had happened to his daughter. A few days after hearing about her death he came to tell me about it. I reminisced with Otto about Anne in spite of the pain it caused me, made worse by the fact that he wept a great deal during our talks. He had been reading the diaries Anne had kept during her enforced confinement in the *Achterhuis* on the Prinsengracht. He had read what Anne had written about me and he knew how close our friendship was. He visited often. It comforted him to know that Anne continued to live in my memory. He regularly invited me to join him in the evening in the city. I didn't enjoy it, but I couldn't bring myself to refuse him. He was curious to know about my life at home and at school as we sat opposite one another in a café, but it never took long before the conversation turned to Anne. I always did my best to fulfil his desire to talk about the subject that most preoccupied him.

On one occasion, probably during the year after the end of the war, he took me with him to the house on the Prinsengracht where he had lived in hiding with his family. It was to become one of Amsterdam's most visited museums in later years, second only to the Rijksmuseum. He showed me the rooms in which Anne had spent all those years behind lock and key. I tried to imagine how he felt as we walked through the empty spaces, which for him were filled with so many sad memories. But beyond being a little less talkative, he managed to conceal his emotions. I saw the blacked-out windows, the tiny kitchen and the Delft blue WC. And I saw the wall that Anne had covered with postcards and pictures of the film stars that had consumed us both. Anne suddenly seemed very close to me. Four years had passed since we cut out those pictures together, but I remembered how much we enjoyed it as if it were yesterday and how we managed to keep the problems that busied the adult world at bay. Anne was dead, but in 1942 death was the farthest thing from our minds. The sight of the wall made the very idea unimaginable once again.

Two of the postcards on the wall were of the English princesses Elizabeth and Margaret Rose. Had she been given them as well, I wondered? My sister and I had received a series of four cards with pictures of the British royal family in 1938 when we were in Paris and the king and queen of England were making an official visit to France. But we used to exchange cards, and when I found one of Shirley Temple in my own collection addressed to Margot Frank, I realised what must have happened. I took a further look at my collection and found what I was looking for, the two remaining cards of the series of four. Were the other two cards now hanging on the wall of the house on the Prinsengracht?

During one of our conversations, Otto Frank – I still called him 'Mr Frank' in those days – told me that he had been advised to publish Anne's diary. He was aware that Anne had thought about publication herself and had already begun to revise the text. She had also devised a title: *Het Achterhuis – The Annexe*. I found it difficult to imagine that anyone would be interested in the stories of a young girl. Otto Frank passed on a request from the publisher, inviting me to write

9

an introduction or epilogue with a few of my own memories but I turned it down. The first edition appeared in 1947 – financed in part by Otto Frank himself – but it sold poorly.

German and French translations appeared in 1950 and the English edition was published in Britain and America in 1952. But it was only after the play based on the book was staged in 1955 and filmed in 1957 that the diary became an international bestseller.

No one knew that Anne had been my friend because I never spoke about the war and my deceased family and friends. I preferred it that way. I didn't want to become the subject of people's interest because of a friend who had been murdered in Bergen-Belsen. When Anne and her diary became world famous, only those closest to me were aware of the fact that she had been my best friend. Anne had referred to me as Jopie in her diary, a name her father had continued to use in the printed version, and a name behind which I was able to hide for many a year.

Following the international success of *Het Achterhuis*, Otto Frank and a number of others established the Anne Frank Foundation in 1957. The Foundation's goal was to fight discrimination, the most harrowing example of which had been the persecution of the Jews, and to promote the ideals Anne had left to the world in her diary. The house on the Prinsengracht, where the eight people Anne describes had gone into hiding, became the Foundation's official address and the building became a museum. It kept Otto exceptionally busy. When he was in Amsterdam for a meeting, he would arrive at our house or telephone us. We wrote to one another regularly and he sent me cards from every corner of the globe. He travelled the world with Anne's diary, which by now had been translated into several languages. I read about it in the newspapers, but never asked him about it and he rarely mentioned it himself. Every now and then I would visit Otto and Fritzi in Basel with my husband Ruud. He lived with his wife in a quiet suburb of the city and liked to hear news about our three children and share stories about Fritzi's grandchildren. I had never met Eva – Fritzi's daughter – who had settled in England a couple of years after the war.

My daughter and her friends had read *Het Achterhuis* by that time, but I had told my children not to mention that Jopie was their mother. My daughter once asked if she could finally tell her best friend about it. Anne had impressed the girl so much and had become her role model. Otto enjoyed talking to the children about Anne and her diary. I even had to encourage my sons to read it before visiting the Franks at the end of one of our vacations. The fact that their mother was mentioned in it embarrassed them slightly.

Without further comment, Otto would always give me copies of new translations of *Het Achterhuis* or other books in which Anne's writings were quoted in one form or another, such as the catalogue of the 1955 *Family of Man* exhibition or *A Passover Haggadah* published in America in 1966 for use during the Seder meal. My diary collection expanded in the years that followed and numbered roughly fifty at its peak. Otto's generosity was his way of involving me in the success of Anne's diary without making a fuss about it.

He also made sure I was invited to Amsterdam if an event was being organised that had something to do with Anne's diary. The first of these visits was in 1956, for a performance of the Dutch translation of the diary's American stage adaptation. Rob de Vries directed and played the role of Otto.

Jetteke, Margot's friend, and I were invited to the premiere, which was also graced by the presence of Queen Juliana. In the middle of the play, I suddenly heard Anne say something about 'Jopie'. It was a strange sensation. My husband and I looked at each other. No one knew I was Jopie. The performance impressed me a great deal, but in spite of the talented actors, I never sensed Anne's presence on the stage. Miep Gies, who had also been invited, told me later she had the same feeling every time she saw a film or theatre piece occasioned by the diary.

I kept the programme, which became the first item in my collection of mementoes and newspaper cuttings on the spectacular ascent Anne's diary enjoyed from then on.

That afternoon, after Otto Frank had allowed me to read the letters Anne had addressed to me in her original diary, we talked about the book *Weerklank – A Tribute to Anne Frank* – edited by Anna G. Steenmeijer. It slowly dawned on me why Anne's diary had become so famous.

Otto was always positive when he spoke to me about the support Anne's diary gave him, and while he hinted on occasion that he was not happy about the mythologisation of his daughter, he had resigned himself to it nevertheless. He realised that the success of the diary had made it inevitable. In spite of the enormous revenue the book had brought him, he continued to live a simple life, determined not to profit financially from the fate of his daughter. The money was placed with the Fund, the Anne Frank Fund in Basel, and set aside for good causes related in one way or another with the ideals Anne had expressed in her diary.

Otto and his second wife travelled the globe to promote

the same ideals. With his daughter's diary at his side as a monument against racial hatred and discrimination, he called for greater understanding between people in the spirit of Anne Frank.

He enjoyed travelling. He was received by kings and presidents, and even by the pope in Rome. Statues of Anne were erected all over the world and countless schools were named after her. Otto was usually present for the unveiling or opening and he would take advantage of the opportunity to speak about his daughter and her diary. It gave new substance to his life. My scrapbook collection contains many a photograph of such events, including some of Otto leading important world rulers around *Het Achterhuis*.

I watched as a Rhine barge slowly made its way upriver. To the left in the distance, a cable ferry made the best of the current to cross from one bank to the other.

I was so deep in thought that I jumped when the telephone rang. It was my sister calling the hotel. Was something wrong with the children? No, Albert, our French uncle, had passed away. His heart, which had long stood up to a lung condition inherited from World War I, had finally given up the ghost.

My sister told me that my mother was planning to travel from Amsterdam to Paris and suggested that I fly to Paris from Basel and accompany her to Uncle Albert's village for the funeral. My sister had to be back in England the following evening and was unable to join us. She was a midwife in a hospital and her holidays were over.

I heard Ruud behind me telephoning the airport to reserve a flight from Basel to Paris.

II

My mother took me to visit her brother Albert a year after the war, and she made the trip a second time alone a couple of months later to discuss inheritance matters, but her visits to the village gradually became less and less frequent. She wanted to avoid further argument about his total neglect of the house. The house was her property. After my grandfather's retirement in the 1920s, he had hinted that the hustle and bustle of Paris was no longer to his taste and my mother had bought the house for her parents even before she married my father. My grandfather had always taken good care of the property and paid his annual taxes and other costs without fail.

Albert had moved in after divorcing his first wife and had lived in the house for years without paying a penny. After the death of his parents, my grandparents, he continued to live there with Jeanne, his second wife, whom he had married shortly after the war, but did nothing to maintain the property. When my mother once passed a remark about the house's sorry decline since their parents' death, he flew into a rage and told her she should pay for the upkeep herself if it bothered her, reminding her that she, after all, was the owner.

My mother saw things differently, of course, especially since he had inherited a tidy sum from their aunt, but she preferred to stay in her brother's good books with a view to the future. While she was irked by the way he had managed to swing the inheritance to his own advantage, he had informed his sister that he would settle matters to her satisfaction in due course and that her daughters would be his beneficiaries.

Although my mother had made up her mind never to set foot in the house in the village again, she advised my sister and me to visit Uncle Albert and Jeanne now and then.

But my grandparents had passed away shortly before the war and, on top of that, the end of the war had opened up an entirely new world for me. During the summer holidays of 1946, I travelled to Oxford and London with a group of schoolmates. The year after that we went to Scotland and by the time we got round to visiting Uncle Albert and Jeanne in 1949, a good three years had passed since my sister and I had last set foot in the village.

We were the only ones to leave the train at the tiny station in the nearest town. Albert was waiting on the platform and we waved excitedly at one another. We jumped into the taxi he had ordered, which brought us to the house where we stayed for a week.

My mother had told us what to expect when we arrived and had made us swear we wouldn't say a word about it. As a result, I pretended not to notice that the walls of the house, which had been whitewashed on a regular basis when my grandparents were still alive, were now grey from years of neglect. The paint on the shutters had flaked off to such a degree that it was hard to tell what colour they had once been. When we climbed the stone stairs to the terrace, I noticed that my grandmother's henhouse was overgrown with weeds. The chickens, which we had fed together each morning in exchange for fresh eggs, had long disappeared.

It was obvious that Jeanne hadn't the slightest inclination to do anything to the house or the terrace. A couple of purple gladioli peered through the abandoned shrubbery, grasping the opportunity to show themselves in spite of the opposition. The gladioli and two rusty folding chairs discarded behind the bushes were the only things that still reminded me of earlier stays. The folding chairs had always been there on the terrace, ready to welcome visitors. My grandfather would sit in one of them to read or peer through his binoculars at Paris in the distance. My sister and I would climb onto them to pick peaches from the tree shading the terrace. We would hold each other for balance, but that wasn't enough to prevent the occasional fall. I once remember my grandmother running out of the house at the sound of my sister's shrieks and how she attended to my bloody knee with a flurry of bandages and sticking plasters. I kept shouting '*C'est pas grave*, it's nothing.' I never liked it when people made a fuss over me.

The peach tree, which was always full of the juiciest peaches, had disappeared from the terrace. When I asked about it, Uncle Albert took it as a reproach and grumbled: 'The tree was never intended to live forever.' I was taken aback by his outburst. He had never spoken to me like that before. Had his conflict with my mother been passed on to us? But he spotted my surprise and added with a grin: '*Citadine*, city girl!'

It goes without saying that we sided with my mother – after all, she had reconciled him with Aunt Julie, my grandfather's sister – but we couldn't simply discard the affection we had always felt towards Uncle Albert, and I was cheered to see that he felt the same way.

My grandfather had been at odds with his sister Julie for

years, unable to accept her frivolous way of life. When it later transpired that her husband had collaborated with the Germans and had died under suspicious circumstances after the war, my uncle refused to have anything more to do with her.

But my mother had spent a number of weeks in Paris taking care of her aunt when she turned out to be incurably ill, partly because she had used her husband's connections to provide my mother with documents during the war that had saved my sister and me from the deportation lists, and partly because my mother expected to inherit a considerable amount from her estate. When she had to leave Paris, she managed to convince Albert to take over from her, the safeguarding of the inheritance being among their primary motives.

When Aunt Julie died a short time later and left her entire estate to Albert, my mother took it for granted that he would share it with her. Her sense of justice and her love for her brother would have inclined her to do the same if she had been the sole beneficiary, but Albert was evidently not convinced.

Jeanne, or *la grosse* – chubby – as my mother invariably called her, lumbered through the front door of the house. My sister and I had seen her once before the war when we visited the *Cirque d'Hiver* with Albert and Jeanne. She kissed us on both cheeks. My mother and grandfather had christened her *la grosse*. They found her dull and were unable to understand what Albert saw in her. Although my grandmother had treated her with kindness, Jeanne had sensed the disapproval of the others and had only returned to the village after the war when she and Albert were married. He had affectionately changed her nickname to *ma grosse*. He was fond of chubby ladies, my mother informed us.

That weekend, my sister and I explored Paris like a couple of tourists. We walked along the famous boulevards, went window-shopping in the legendary shops and were amazed at the amount of traffic and the crowded streets and pavement cafés. We took the metro from one place of interest to the next. We visited Napoleon's grave and saw the *Mona Lisa* in the Louvre. And, of course, we climbed the Eiffel Tower. We lunched in those cheap little restaurants in the Quartier Latin where the waiters can balance six plates on one arm as they manoeuvre their way between the tightly packed tables. I made a frequent point of popping into the second-hand bookshops in the student district where I inhaled the typical smell of musty old books, which I recognised from my father's library at our house on Willemsparkweg in Amsterdam. Pocket-sized hand-bound editions cost next to nothing and I indulged myself.

They say that when the metro is packed to the gunnels and the people are all squeezed in together, girls are regularly targeted by men who can't keep their hands to themselves. We can confirm it. When it happened to us we just looked the other way and blushed, in contrast to a *Parisienne* we once heard seriously lambasting her assailant and forcing him to get off at the next station red with shame, the disdainful looks of the female passengers and the sniggers of the men launching him onto the platform.

We returned to Uncle Albert's late in the afternoon tired from our escapades. A huge bowl of salad had been prepared for us and Albert made steak and potatoes with garlic. Jeanne didn't eat with us. She busied herself in the kitchen with her own treats, stirring with gusto, her chubby fingers wrapped around a wooden spoon. Albert spoiled her and did all the shopping. She did nothing in the house. She got up late and took an extra nap after lunch, and came down from her nap bright and breezy in her floral dress. She had clearly been styling her auburn hair and had draped a semi-circular curl over her temples left and right. She confided that she used sugared water to make sure it stayed in place. Every table and cupboard in the house was buried under piles of paper and other bits and pieces, but it didn't seem to bother her or Albert.

They were a happy couple with their little dog Toutou at their side. It was clear that they were content in the village house. Albert worked in the vegetable garden in the mornings and headed off to the local bistro at the end of the day as he had done for years on end. Before the inheritance, Albert had worked in *La Samaritaine* – a major department store in Paris – but he had since given up the job and completely assimilated himself to life in the village and its farming residents. He wore sleeveless blue dungarees or *salopettes* all day long and a flat cap if the sun was too fierce. I tried to imagine what my mother would think of this metamorphosis. Her brother had always been so elegantly dressed. I decided not to tell her. During their walks with Toutou, Jeanne also came into contact with the rest of the villagers, but she never received anyone at home.

I missed my grandmother's beautiful sideboard. Jeanne had exchanged it for a vulgar kitchen cabinet that now stood where the sideboard used to be and was entirely out of place. I pretended it was the most natural thing in the world, a kitchen cabinet in the living room, and did my utmost not to look at it. But I couldn't help thinking of my grandmother's blackcurrant jam that had always adorned the now absent sideboard. In spite of the fact that almost all of the furniture had been left undisturbed, the room no longer matched what I remembered of it. But I did remember the bowls Albert now used to serve our morning coffee, and the croissant we dunked in it tasted just the same as before.

It was busy in the village that week. It was the annual fair and we met all the old faces on the main street, including one of the boys I had danced with several times on a visit to the village with my mother a couple of years earlier, when the liberation festivities were still in full swing. He and his wife were pushing a pram. Albert looked into it and said reproachfully: 'That could have been your baby.' He confided that the boy in question had indeed asked on several occasions when I would be coming back for a visit.

We also bumped into an old girlfriend. Chantal had since married a boy from a neighbouring village and was expecting her first child.

Several years were to pass before I was to return to the village. I had met my own husband in the meantime and had three children, but when they were a little older we would take them for a visit to Albert and Jeanne now and then. Albert was always delighted to see us and he treated our children as if they were his own grandchildren. He even took his new *neveu* – as he called Ruud – with him to the local bistro where he introduced him to his *copains*, as he had my father before him, and they downed a glass of *eau-de-vie* after dinner.

Albert found Ruud's excellent French – due in part to his conversations with my mother – nothing out of the ordinary. His own knowledge of English had faded over the years, although he still boasted that he had learned the language during a brief stay in the local seminary. I once saw him produce a handkerchief from his pocket and tell the children that 'those crazy Englishmen' called the thing an *ant-ker-chief*. He pronounced the word with a very heavy and very explicit French accent. Given the fact that he never went anywhere – he had never been to Holland to see his sister and never would – his own language was enough for him. And like the majority of French people in those days, he thought that everyone should speak French; in his eyes it was a universal language. Jeanne and the children understood one another without words. She would always make them *crème caramel*. My daughter liked it, but I had to make the boys pretend it was a special treat and they ended up with the same gooey pudding on the next visit.

We never stayed with them. They were both too old and wouldn't have been up to it. On top of that, the house's decline had pressed ahead with a vengeance. The rugs had disappeared and the linoleum was so tattered and worn out you could see the floorboards beneath it. A brand-new roll of linoleum had been standing in a corner of the room for years. Several different items had also disappeared from the house as time passed, including the bronze mantelpiece set. A mantel clock had appeared in its place with two porcelain seagulls above, their wings spread triumphantly. Because I no longer ventured upstairs, I was unable to check whether the mantelpiece set had found its way to the bedroom fireplace and whether the paintings my father had given his in-laws had been relocated to the upper floor. They had long made way for weeping children, sultry provocative gipsy women and a tapestry with what passed for an alpine meadow, now sagging in its twisted frame, its folds full of dust. In the middle of it all hung a calendar that was years out of date. Clothes and newspapers were piled up on every chair and the tables and cupboards were covered and stuffed with papers, boxes, and all sorts of bits and bobs that had just been left lying there after they had been used. Toutou had died a couple of years earlier, but his collar and leash, and sacks of dog food were still in the kitchen cabinet in the living room. It was a good thing that my mother had decided not to come back to the place.

The first thing my mother noticed when we climbed the stone stairs was that Toutou had been buried on the terrace. The discovery horrified her. She hadn't been to the house in the village for decades.

The door was wide open and we went inside. The shutters were closed. We found Jeanne surrounded by chaos in the semi-darkness of the living room. She was sitting at the table, her chin in her hands, crushed. She looked up when we came into the room, her eyes filled with tears. To her left, resting diagonally across the table – which had been partly cleared for the occasion – was the coffin with Albert's remains. She had asked permission to keep the coffin open until her sister-in-law arrived to give her the chance to see her brother one last time. My mother hadn't been looking forward to it, but she went through the motions and looked inside the coffin. I waited by the door and wondered how they were going to get the coffin through the gate at the bottom of the stone stairs. The gate was so covered in rust that it refused to open more than halfway. They had brought the coffin in on its end but there was no alternative to carrying it out horizontally. The solution turned out to be relatively simple: they lifted the gate off its hinges.

The service in the old village church was done with

style. Jeanne had asked the parish priest for the maximum number of altar servers and choir boys. The scent of incense filled the air. The mass took forever. I suddenly realised that there were two empty spaces in the church behind the altar. The two sixteenth-century wooden statues, the pride of the entire village, had disappeared. I pointed it out to Chantal who was sitting beside me. She told me they had been stolen from the church a couple of years earlier.

After the service we walked behind the bier, passing the house on the way to the old cemetery. Many of the villagers joined us. Albert had clearly endeared himself among the villagers in the years he had lived in their midst. All those present sprinkled the coffin with holy water at the cemetery and Albert was interred in the family vault next to his parents.

On the way back we passed the vegetable garden where my grandfather and later Albert had worked with such pleasure. The sight of it saddened me. I was reminded of our annual summer holidays in the village, before the war, when my grandparents were still alive and its presence had contributed to the unforgettable times my sister and I had enjoyed there as children.

Jeanne snivelled all the way.

'Be strong, you have to be strong,' my mother told her repeatedly. She didn't exhibit the slightest emotion herself, and I knew she was worried about the inheritance. I was horrified when she suddenly raised the subject.

'I imagine Albert will have made the necessary arrangements for the inheritance?' she asked Jeanne.

'Albert was quite content to leave that all up to me,' Jeanne answered, affronted. 'And I'll settle matters in due course.' She said afterwards that she wanted to stay in the house, and my mother, wisely avoiding the subject of the inheritance, was quick to assure her that she could stay as long as she pleased. It was now her sister-in-law who required careful handling.

When we said our goodbyes, Jeanne said tearfully: 'You'll still come and visit, won't you, even now that Albert's gone?'

My mother told her sister-in-law that she didn't feel up to travelling at her age. That wasn't exactly true since she still visited her old friend Germaine every year in those days and didn't mind the trip to Compiègne. The year before she had even managed to clamber unharmed out of Germaine's empty swimming pool after falling into it backwards no less. She was seventy-eight years old. Apart from a couple of bruises she was right as rain. Her friendship with Germaine dated back to the time they both worked for a fashion house in Paris and before my mother set off in the twenties to continue her fashion career in Amsterdam. They kept in touch, even after she and my father got married.

My mother couldn't face the state of the house and knew she wouldn't be able to hold her tongue about it if she came back so she sought an excuse. The important thing was to secure the inheritance for her daughters and she wanted to avoid getting into an argument with her sister-in-law at all costs. She found Jeanne stupid and ugly, two characteristics she despised the most in people. She also didn't understand why I had a soft spot for Jeanne, but was delighted when I volunteered to visit her now and then.

I travelled to Paris twice a year in those days, where I followed summer courses in bookbinding, and it gave me the opportunity to make good on my promise to Jeanne. I usually took a box of Belgian bonbons with me, but when I forgot them one year and brought her a bouquet of roses instead she couldn't find a vase. She gave me a plastic water bottle and a pair of scissors and asked me to cut off the top. We used the rest of the bottle as a vase for the roses.

    My sister continued to send Jeanne a letter every now and then from England. My mother limited herself to the obligatory greeting card around New Year. We were all quite taken aback when she replied in magnificent handwriting.

III

12 June 1979 was a day that didn't pass unnoticed. It would have been Anne's fiftieth birthday. I took my place in the Westerkerk among the many other invited guests and listened to the various speeches and the songs that had been chosen to fit the occasion. I could see Anne's father from where I was sitting. How did he feel, I wondered? Had he grown accustomed by now to the idea that his daughter had come to symbolise the millions of Jews murdered by the Nazis? I imagined, on reflection, that he took some satisfaction in the fact that her writings continued to confront people with the persecution of the Jews. The goal of the Foundation set up in her name was to maintain awareness of the consequences of racism and discrimination.

I was reminded of a sentence I came across in one of her stories, a collection of which had been published in the meantime in several languages: 'One way or another, people will know my name in the future.' Now everyone did indeed know her name. But in my thoughts I pictured a young girl celebrating her thirteenth birthday and enjoying being the centre of attention at the party she had organised for her classmates. She wrote about it in the diary she had received from her parents the day before. I gave her a book called *Dutch Sagas and Legends* because she had enjoyed my *Myths and Legends of Greece and Rome* so much. We read a lot together, and often shared the same books. I still have the book she gave me on my own birthday, safe in my small collection of tangible memories of Anne.

During the reception that followed, Otto Frank made his way over to me. 'I want you to meet someone,' he said. 'You were one of the first people I went to when I learned that Anne was dead. This is the woman who was with Anne when she died, the woman I told you about back then.' It was one of the sisters from Rotterdam who had worked as nurses in the camp and had seen both the Frank sisters die, first Margot then Anne. I shook her hand and nodded politely, but I didn't say anything. I had nothing to add to all the wonderful words that had already been said that afternoon.

German television took the opportunity of Anne's fiftieth birthday to make a documentary about her. It seemed good to me that programmes about the Nazi period should be broadcast in Germany – the American film *Holocaust* was being screened worldwide at the time and had occasioned much discussion of the persecution of the Jews and their fate under the Nazis, especially in Germany. I agreed to participate in the documentary on Otto Frank's explicit request, although I still preferred to avoid publicity at the time whenever possible. He was scheduled to feature in the documentary himself and Miep Gies had also agreed to participate.

The interviews for the documentary were edited between recordings of rehearsals for a performance of the play *Het Achterhuis* by a group of German schoolchildren. While watching the video, a young girl, perhaps eighteen years of age, made a remark about the persecution of the Jews: 'Why did no one tell us about this? Does this make our parents a bunch of liars?' This question alone made me glad that I had participated in the documentary. I also knew that no one in the Netherlands would get to see it and that my appearance on television would go unnoticed.

A short segment of film with moving pictures of Anne, which was only later to arouse my curiosity, was edited into the documentary.

On the occasion of the revival of the play *Het Achterhuis* in 1983, I was invited by Hanneke Groenteman to give a radio interview. I was excited that the play was returning to the stage, this time under the direction of Jeroen Krabbé, who was also to play Otto Frank. I answered a few questions for the microphone under the name 'Jopie'.

On 20 August 1980, I heard a newsreader on the radio announce: 'Otto Frank, father of the internationally renowned diarist Anne Frank, has died in his home in Basel.'

He was ninety years old. We had visited him in Basel only a month earlier. There had been rumours of pleurisy, but it turned out to be lung cancer. I knew when I saw him that it would be the last time. He was lying on the sofa in a room off the living room and was terribly weak. He was pleased to see us, but the ever kind and optimistic man was tired. He shared his disappointment with us at what he had established with such idealism. Too much had slipped from his hands over the years and he had been forced to endure too much criticism. Jewish circles in particular accused him of drawing too much attention to his daughter and himself. He was scheduled to visit the hospital the following day to have his lungs drained of fluid, but he made it clear to us that he didn't want to go.

The Anne Frank Foundation had arranged airline tickets. Miep Gies had added me to the list of people planning to attend the memorial service in Basel.

After the service, our party made its way to a nearby restaurant for lunch. The convivial and upbeat atmosphere bothered me, as did the copious lunch some ordered and the amount of wine that was consumed. I hadn't yet grown accustomed to the fact that the Anne Frank Foundation had become a business undertaking and the use of its funds was not only confined to the promotion of its honourable goals. I ate a sandwich and had time over to walk to the Tingeuly fountain with two women from the group.

In the afternoon, I joined Fritzi Frank and a number of people from the Foundation at her home. She introduced me to a Swiss acquaintance: 'This is Jopie.' *'Oh das ganze Tagebuch ist hier* – the entire diary is here,' she exclaimed. 'Only the ones who didn't die,' I said with a knowing glance intended for Miep Gies who was standing within earshot.

Fritzi took me to one side. 'I was planning to play a recording of Otto, but I don't want to interrupt the conversations.'

'Otto is why we're here,' I answered.

Moments later we listened to the voice of Otto Frank telling us the story of his life in words he had used at a recent visit to a school in Basel. I had heard and read his curriculum vitae on more than one occasion, but the pride with which he spoke of his days as an officer in the German army suddenly struck me at that moment. He had served during World War I, before the Nazi period, but I found it difficult to understand that he could be proud of serving a country that had caused him so much suffering. He must have felt more German than Jewish in those days, I imagined, like so many other disillusioned German Jews.

When we arrived home that evening, I noticed that all the newspapers were carrying reports of the events in Basel.

I also maintained contact with Fritzi after Otto's death and we exchanged letters every now and then. She had become a member of the Anne Frank Foundation's Board of Trustees in the meantime and made regular visits to the Netherlands. She usually came for dinner when she was in town.

In May 1982, two years after the death of Otto Frank, the Anne Frank Foundation celebrated its twenty-fifth anniversary. I was invited to a meeting being organised at the Anne Frank House in Amsterdam. As always my thoughts returned to Anne and how she would have revelled in all this attention. I shared them on the spur of the moment with one of the Foundation's governors, a woman I had met two years earlier in Basel at the memorial ceremony for Otto when we went for a walk to the Tingeuly fountain. She was clearly put out by my words and said: 'We shouldn't only think about Anne. So many other children died.' I didn't respond. I had encountered similar reactions often enough, but her remark was not exactly what I would have expected from one of the Anne Frank Foundation's governors. Surely she was aware that the suffering of so many children had been made real in the person of Anne? And surely it was appropriate to think about that if only for a moment, in this house, on this day, with Anne's name constantly on everyone's lips.

Miep and Jan Gies always attended these meetings and we bumped into each other on a regular basis. I knew there were those who thought that Miep and Jan Gies were the subject of too much attention. They sometimes received unpleasant letters from people who disapproved of all the interest being devoted to Miep when so many others had done good things during the war. As luck would have it, Miep had helped Anne Frank and she too had become a symbol, a symbol for those who found ethical norms and laws more important than the laws enforced by the Nazis, even at the risk of their own lives.

In the meantime, the Anne Frank Foundation had organised a travelling exhibition entitled *The World of Anne Frank*. The exhibition charted the consequences of racism and discrimination with the use of photos and video testimonies and was opened to the public for the first time in Amsterdam in 1985. Lin Jaldati, the stage name of the woman Otto Frank had introduced me to that day in the Westerkerk, the woman who had been present with her sister in Bergen-Belsen when first Margot and then Anne succumbed to illness, sang Yiddish songs together with her husband and daughters. She performed a fragment of her theatre production *For Anne Frank* in which she spoke about Anne and Margot's final hours. I was horrified to hear that Anne had spent her last days staggering around the camp in ice-cold temperatures with nothing but a blanket to protect her. She had thrown away the rags she had been wearing up to that point in disgust. They were infested with lice.

The Queen also attended the opening in Amsterdam. Anne would have been delighted that I had met the Queen because of *her* book.

In 1987, I received a report from America that a film crew was on its way to the Netherlands to make a film about Anne and they asked if I would be willing to participate. Hannah, referred to in Anne's diary as Lies, was also scheduled to be interviewed for the documentary. I hesitated at first, but Hannah's participation was enough to win me over.

We spent our summer holidays in Italy that year and that is where the interviews took place. They also wanted me to accompany them to various places in Amsterdam associated with Anne, but had to wait until my return two weeks later.

There I was, standing in front of Anne's house on the

Merwedeplein for the first time in forty-five years. The woman who now lived in the house directed us to a small side room. 'This was Anne's room,' she said. I didn't remember it. We usually played in the living room where we also did our homework. I still remembered the living room and I also remembered a room off the living room in which Anne's grandmother would sit in the corner by the window overlooking the square below. The kitchen was exactly the same as before. I stared at the corner of the worktop where Anne always prepared her sandwiches after school and where the cat Moortje would circle around her begging for something to eat.

It suddenly dawned on me as we left the house. Anne's unmade bed and the new shoes with the wooden soles the day Hannah and I visited the abandoned house of the Frank family, the day after they disappeared. The picture was engraved in my memory. I imagined Anne sitting on the bed and kicking off the shoes when her father told her she couldn't take them with her. The bed was against the wall to the right of the door. There was a different bed there now. That was Anne's room, the bigger room at the back on the right-hand side. Perhaps Anne had started in the smaller room – although I can't remember it – and had changed rooms after her grandmother died in January 1942. I also presumed that Otto had visited the house on the Merwedeplein after the war from time to time and that he must have explained how the various rooms had been allocated.

We walked with the camera crew from the Merwedeplein to the house in which I used to live in Hunzestraat. On the way we passed the bookshop where Anne's first diary – the chequered one – had been purchased and where we always bought our books and other school supplies. I pointed to the massive Hebrew letters on the façade of the synagogue on Lekstraat, which amazingly enough had survived the war. When we arrived in Hunzestraat I spoke about Miep and Jan Gies who lived opposite us and pointed to their house. I also spoke of the many Jewish neighbours I had seen rounded up and taken away.

We then moved on to the building on the other side of the River Amstel where the Jewish Lyceum had been accommodated during the war and which all the Jewish children had been obliged to attend. From the beginning of the school year in 1941, normal schools were no longer open to Jewish pupils. We arrived at the schoolyard. Memories that had etched themselves in my mind – whether I wanted it or not – flooded back. The schoolyard, which had bustled with chattering and laughing children at the beginning of the year, had grown emptier as the year went on. I didn't recognise the classrooms. The old benches had been replaced with new ones, but the gymnasium was the same as before. I spoke about the school and the year I had spent there with Anne. Once we were outside, I mentioned that Anne had had to be excused from certain exercises in the gym because she had once dislocated her shoulder. The director asked me to tell the same story in the gym itself, this time for the camera. Hannah had also said something about Anne's shoulder and my story could be edited in after Hannah's testimony.

After the film crew had left I lost my voice for three days in a row, given up the ghost as a result of too much talking, I presumed. Although the documentary was never completed, it had occasioned an uninterrupted and detailed confrontation with the past that was new to me. It was not to be the last time that I would take the 'tourist route' from the

Merwedeplein to the school, but at that moment I decided to put an end to my involvement in such ventures. As time had passed I had agreed more often to participate, primarily to confirm the authenticity of the diary – which was sometimes open to debate in those days – but also because I thought it right that I should be there when others like Miep and Hannah were telling their stories.

It turned out otherwise. Certain developments drew me more and more into the public eye and plunged me into a conflict that was to last for years and which was doomed never to be resolved.

It started in 1986, the year in which Anne's collected writings were published by the *Rijksinstituut voor Oorlogsdocumentatie* (RIOD) – now called NIOD, Netherlands Institute for War Documentation – and six years after the death of Otto Frank.

I found it difficult at first to understand the need to publically expose all of Anne's intimate outpourings, and I have to admit that most of the passages I had in mind had to do with me, passages I still found painful. Similarly, Anne's descriptions of her classmates, which her father had let me read, did not seem publishable to me and were a humiliation for many of those who had died in the war. I wrote a letter to the RIOD informing them that I did not agree with their publication. I was unaware at the time that Anne had also made less than flattering references to adults in her writings, especially her mother and Pfeffer, the dentist who had joined the family in hiding in the *Achterhuis*.

A few days later, I read in the paper that Anne's handwriting was to be scrutinised by experts together with the paper and the sort of ink she had used. It went without saying that the paper and ink had to have been manufactured prior to the date inscribed in Anne's writings. The handwriting in Anne's diary was to be compared with letters she had written around the same period, including one to her grandmother in Switzerland. The New Year greetings card Anne had sent me in January 1942 and the poem she had written in my poetry album on 23 March of the same year were also to be used. The postage stamp and postmark on the card were included as evidence of authenticity.

Anne's collected writings, entitled *The Diary of Anne Frank: The Critical Edition*, thus appeared in a version intended to demonstrate their authenticity. Neo-Nazi's had contested the diary as documentary confirmation of the Holocaust through the years and Otto Frank had taken the matter to court on more than one occasion.

The new authenticated version included the three existing versions of the diary in order to avoid further confusion. The first version is the original diary Anne started to write on her thirteenth birthday. After a while she decided to copy and rework it with the intention of publishing it in book form after the war. She added notes and commentary stemming from a variety of different dates to this second version. She expanded some parts, abbreviated others, and introduced name changes. She referred to me as 'Jopie' in this version, which was still incomplete on the day the family were arrested. The third version is a selection of texts made by Otto Frank from his daughter's writings and represents the first published edition of the diary dating from 1947. Otto Frank had made a small number of corrections to this text prior to publication. Although Anne had learned to speak good Dutch in the preceding years, German was still spoken at home with her mother and family friends. As a consequence, her writings were peppered with the odd Germanism. Otto also removed certain fragments to protect the good name of those who may have been subject to one of Anne's not so equally kind descriptions. The original publisher also asked him to leave out the passages in which Anne had spoken about the changes that were taking place in her body.

When I was informed that completeness was of the greatest importance in establishing the authenticity of the writings and testimonies and was invited to collaborate in the project, I finally overcame my objections and agreed to reveal my identity. The first version of the diary, the version Anne had not yet revised, contained my name in full, and this was to be made public for the first time.

Fritzi was also against a comprehensive edition at first. She was convinced that Otto would not have wanted it and she managed to have some of Anne's remarks withdrawn from the manuscript, especially unpleasant passages about her mother.

Awkward passages about her parents' marriage were also included in the five pages of diary that surfaced out of the blue in 1998. I was not convinced it had much to contribute to what we already knew from Anne's existing writings. Anne had already devoted an entry in her diary to one of the stories in her Story Book called 'Caddy's Life', in which the main character continues to adore his lost love, decades after they part. She writes: 'This is not sentimental rubbish, because it incorporates the novel of Father's life.' Beyond this we can only guess how much of the story squared with reality. The marriage between Otto Frank and Edith Holländer was probably arranged, as was often the case among better off Jewish families. But I was familiar with the evasive answers Anne's father had dished up in response to her curious questions about sexuality, and I wondered whether Otto had not told his daughter a slightly romanticised story of his own life to oblige her curiosity and romantic sensitivities.

A new version of *Het Achterhuis* or *The Diary of a Young Girl*, as it was known in English, was published a good ten years after Otto Frank's death, a fourth version edited – according to the title page – by Otto Frank and Mirjam Pressler. This version includes segments Anne had quite consciously removed, but the additions do not always give a clear picture of her thoughts because the remarks she wrote between the lines are not included. She would certainly have distanced herself from this version, because it does not take her own reworking of the text seriously.

David Barnouw, a member of staff at the NIOD, wrote in his 1998 collection of essays on 'Anne Frank the Myth' entitled *Anne Frank voor beginners en gevorderden – Anne Frank for Beginners and Beyond*: 'The NIOD edition was used to produce a "new" *Achterhuis*, a publication referred to as *The Definitive Edition* without the slightest justification. Why a new *Achterhuis*? The Anne Frank Fund in Basel feared that copyrights on the "old" *Achterhuis* and its various translations would lapse fifty years after the death of the author. This would mean that anyone could republish the book without being obliged to pay a penny to the Fund (…) Although copyright had been extended in the meantime to seventy years, the Fund still felt the need to take action. It commissioned German author Mirjam Pressler, the translator of the German NIOD edition, to put together a "comprehensive" *Achterhuis*, partly on the basis of newly published material. A "new" *Achterhuis* thus appeared in 1991, with

Otto Frank (who had been dead for more than ten years) and Mirjam Pressler as its editors. This meant that copyright on the material would only lapse seventy years after the death of Otto Frank and Mirjam Pressler, and far into the twenty-first century. Can we then expect a "new" *Definitive Edition?*'

This fourth edition completely eclipsed the original edition compiled by Otto Frank and published in 1947. The only place the original version still appears to be available is the United States, where it continues to be used extensively in schools.

IV

I spoke to Ruud for the first time on a ferry on its way to England shortly after the war with a group from my school. He was part of another group of young people making the same trip. I recognised him as the neighbour's boy who had spent the war in hiding and had reappeared in our neighbourhood after the war was over. I bought a new bicycle in England with the money my father asked me to collect from a business acquaintance with whom he traded in prints. Bicycles were still difficult to come by in the Netherlands and my purchase attracted a lot of attention from my fellow passengers. Ruud's organisational talent was already apparent even then. When we arrived back in Amsterdam he suggested that he would put me on the tram with our baggage and he would cycle home on my new bike. I had been looking forward to cycling through the city again for the first time in years, and of course, *he* could have accompanied the baggage on the tram, but I understood that the thought of cycling through Amsterdam was what had inspired his offer and I said nothing about it. It would have been impossible to fit my suitcase on the back of the bicycle. He put on a bit of a spurt and was already waiting for me at the tram stop on Rijnstraat when the tram arrived.

He had fallen in love in England with a pretty blonde girl but had been too shy to say anything to her. A couple of days after we got back he appeared elated at my door with a letter from her and he let me read it. 'Do you think she's in love with me too?' he asked once I'd finished reading. If what I later heard from him was anything to go by, a lively correspondence ensued and continued for quite some time. We both had our own circle of friends in those days and only bumped into each other on the street every once in a while.

Final year secondary students in 1945 were granted their school leaving certificate without having to take any exams. The education system had also suffered during the war and this was taken into account in the first few years after the war was over. In other words, the exams were less strict. In 1948, however, they unexpectedly returned to normal and the final exams at the Girls' Lyceum ended in a fiasco. Half of our class failed, including my girlfriend Grietje and myself. I decided the time had come to leave school, and although my parents – especially my father – were disappointed about it, they had their own worries and weren't entirely unhappy at the idea of some extra income. I learned to type during the summer, qualified as a stenographer in Dutch, French, German and English, and attended classes in business correspondence in the same languages. I picked up a secretarial job in the meantime in the offices of a Jewish wine merchant. This went down particularly well with my father who saw it as a sign that I had not completely abandoned the Jewish faith. But the real reason I had applied for the job was because it gave me both Saturdays and Sundays off, which was quite unusual in those days.

I still lived with my parents, but when an ex-school friend wrote to me from London in 1952 asking if I wanted to take over her au pair job I immediately jumped at the chance to get away from the suffocating atmosphere at home.

The problems that had reached their lowest ebb during the war on account of my parents' mixed marriage had established an enormous gulf between them. My mother couldn't forgive my father for putting us in danger by registering us in the Jewish community in Amsterdam in 1938. Although he had heard about what was going on in Nazi Germany from German Jews who had fled to the Netherlands, his estimation of the violent spread of Nazism throughout Europe had been too optimistic. Fortunately, my mother had been able to have the registration annulled in 1942 by storming into the lion's den – the *Sicherheitsdienst* or SD in Amsterdam's Euterpestraat – in her Easter best and informing the Germans that she was actually a French Catholic and that her two daughters were not Jewish. Her husband, she said, had registered her children in the Jewish community before the war without her knowledge. The Germans were impressed by her determination and told her that her children would be removed from the deportation list if she could prove that her French grandparents were non-Jewish. It took some doing to acquire copies of her grandparents' birth and baptismal certificates from the unoccupied part of France but she managed it.

My sister and I thus found ourselves in an extraordinary situation in the middle of the occupation: suddenly we were no longer Jews and even my father was allowed to remove the star from his clothing a few months later. My mother, my sister and I weren't much inclined to become Jewish once again after the war, but my father retreated more and more into the Jewish faith as the years passed and he met with his friends every day at the synagogue. My parents argued like cat and dog at the beginning, but their arguments gradually gave way to a steely silence. My sister left home shortly afterwards to follow a course in midwifery at a hospital in Manchester.

The couple I lived with in England had a three-year-old

daughter and it was my job to look after her. The mother was a writer of children's books and the father an editor with the *New Statesman*.

I enjoyed my time in London. I had plenty of contact with the other Dutch au pairs and they introduced me to their foreigners' club where we met on a regular basis. I got to know a Swiss boy at the club after he tossed a cup of coffee over my dress. As a result of his clumsiness we ended up going out on the town together every now and then. He had been working for a company in London for some time and knew his way around. He told me later that he had mentioned the coffee incident in a letter to his parents and that his father had advised him to ask me out if he liked me and to compensate for the dress if he didn't. I might have made a different choice if he'd told me earlier on. Ruud and I kept in touch by letter in those days and when I wrote about the incident he was clearly jealous, although he had no reason to be.

My employers did their best to include me in their family circle. On a number of occasions, the master of the house asked me if I was interested in the complementary tickets that were regularly handed in to the editorial offices of the *New Statesman*, inviting reviews of various theatre performances in the city. He suggested I come and collect them from his office in town, but I never took him up on the offer. His wife seemed a little ill at ease when he took notice of me.

He arrived home one day with a book that had been submitted to the *New Statesman* for review and said: 'This was written by a Dutch girl. Maybe you'd like to read it.' It was *The Diary of a Young Girl*, the first English edition of *Het Achterhuis*, and the Dutch girl was Anne Frank. Although I had read Anne's diary five years earlier and this was my second reading, I was surprised to find that the English edition contained Anne's description of the time she suggested we feel each other's breasts as a sign of our friendship. The English edition clearly differed from the Dutch on a number of points and the latter had made no mention of my breasts. The description alludes to a 'friend' and doesn't mention my name, but I remembered the incident as if it was yesterday and I was taken aback to read about it. I was moved as I read further. Immediately after her account of the episode Anne writes in her diary 'she refused', true to reality. It turned out later that my name had in fact been mentioned in the original version. I was grateful to Otto Frank for removing it when he read the English translation of Anne's diary prior to publication.

I didn't tell my employer when he gave me the book that I was 'Jopie', one of the characters, and I still wasn't sure whether I should tell him after I had read it. A girlfriend of the lady of the house was staying with them at the time and we regularly sat by the fire reading together. When I asked her if she would like to read the book after I had finished it, she looked at me disapprovingly, curled her lips and said no. My story remained untold. I was hypersensitive about anti-Semitism in those days, a lingering remnant from the war years, and it continued to play tricks on me.

Not long afterwards, my mother telephoned to tell me that my father had died suddenly. His heart problem finally caught up with him. He had been poorly for some time and had been unable to rebuild his business. His print-collecting hobby had become his livelihood and he and my mother, who was now a seamstress – a word she detested – managed quite well on their combined incomes. I travelled to Amsterdam the following day.

I realised at the funeral how many friends my father had in the Jewish community. They helped carry the coffin. After the recitation of a liturgical text in the auditorium and a word of remembrance from one of his friends, we followed the coffin to the cemetery and the grave.

His death came unexpectedly. I felt sad, to some extent because I was aware of my shortcomings towards him at home. My eagerness to avoid my parents' problems meant that I had also avoided *his* problems. On top of that, none of his family had returned from the camps after the war and I had never taken the time to talk to him about it.

My mother told me later that she was pleased when I cried all the way to the cemetery and that it had been good for the family name. She had apparently managed to keep a dry eye throughout.

Each of the men, Ruud included, pitched three shovelfuls of earth on top of the coffin. Gerard, still Van het Reve in those days, did the same. He came to visit us year after year with his wife Hannie and a violinist who had made the acquaintance of my mother after the war. The violinist, referred to invariably by Gerard as Mrs Polak-Daniels although her real name was De Boer, befriended Hannie who had been left destitute and parentless by the war. My mother also concerned herself with Hannie's fate, as she did with others who had returned from the camps or come out of hiding. She even made her wedding dress. I hadn't seen Gerard for some time, but I knew he had a fondness for funerals and had once considered becoming Jewish. He and my father spoke about it a great deal.

In the course of the years, I had overheard my father saying to my mother on a number of occasions that he didn't believe she would light a memorial candle for him – a prescribed Jewish ritual – after his death, but he had been mistaken. The candle was kept lit for a full year.

I didn't return to England. The child I had been given charge of was difficult and with winter on its way I wasn't looking forward to the long walks I would have to take with her. My English had improved considerably during my six months in England, and that, after all, was the reason for my stay.

I didn't want to commit myself to a particular job in those days so I found secretarial work in Amsterdam via an agency and always refused offers of permanent employment. I had given up my business correspondence classes and did little more that winter than enjoy the nightlife with my girlfriends, especially the cinema. After an absence of six months, I realised how beautiful Amsterdam was all of a sudden and I was happy to be back.

Ruud bought his first boat that spring, and he asked me if I would like to go sailing with him on Westeinderplas Lake. He had forgotten all about his crush on the blonde girl and he now divided his attention between his boat and his dark-haired sailing companion.

Ruud and I got engaged in the same year, 1953, and the two-week summer vacation we had in those days was entirely devoted to sailing on Westeinderplas Lake. I never became a sailing fanatic.

We married in 1954 and our daughter was born in 1956 in Brussels where Ruud had been despatched by his employer for two years. Our two sons were born after we returned to the Netherlands and our sailing holidays moved to the Ijsselmeer.

Our three children demanded all my attention for several years. I picked up what I needed to know about babies and toddlers from the then famous book by Dr Spock and I read *Magriet*, a woman's weekly, determined as I was to be a good mother and housewife in spite of my natural inclinations to the contrary. I devoted myself completely to raising my children and didn't plan to go back to work as my own mother had done. That would have been exceptional in those days. None of the women I knew had a job in addition to household duties.

I washed, shopped, cooked, took the children to school in the morning, collected them in the afternoon, and brought them to their sport activities, music lessons, and friends. I was a member of the parents' committee at both primary and secondary school. Fortunately all three of the children attended the same Montessori primary and Vossius Grammar when they were older. My mother-in-law thought I was overprotective, but when our family doctor once complimented me for the way I was raising the children my sense of being a successful housewife was immediately complete.

Every Friday evening my mother, mother-in-law and entourage would come to our house for dinner whether my husband was away on business or not. I found it enormously taxing, especially because I was determined to show that I had become the perfect Dutch housewife, something my own mother had never been and my mother-in-law had doubted in the early years of our marriage. But it had become an expectation and that was that. It never dawned on me to protest.

As a consequence, and by the time my daughter was old enough for secondary school and my sons were ten and six, my intellectual life had, to all intents and purposes, reached rock bottom. So many years living at the level of my children started to take their toll and I decided to leave them with my mother every now and then, although her pedagogical skills weren't exactly to be overestimated. As far as my mother was concerned, most children were difficult, stupid and ugly, but for some reason her prejudices didn't apply to her own three grandchildren. To her they were the height of intelligence and beauty. They loved her and respected her enormously, but she let them do whatever they wanted when they were with her and it always took me a full day to get them back under control.

The art classes I took at Amsterdam's Volksuniversiteit – a sort of Open University – were organised in the evenings. I would wash up quickly after dinner, put the children to bed and head off. If Ruud was out of town on business, which was often the case, my mother would babysit.

The legendary Mrs s'Jacob whose classes I attended had earned her reputation among Amsterdam's lovers of art history. With the help of a collection of slides, she presented a well-ordered survey of the entire history of art since time immemorial, conveniently arranged in weekly classes spread over a period of six years. She was eighty in those days and had reduced the course to four years to be on the safe side. I was always tired when I left the house, but by the time I got back I was wide awake and I would usually spend a couple of hours looking up what I had seen and heard that evening in the books I had bought on the subject. Having set aside my own interests for so many years to be able to raise my children, I was particularly receptive to learning new things. The classes in French literature I followed a couple of years later at the Institut Français in Amsterdam were just the same. The programme still lead to Sorbonne exams in those days, which I took with success.

One of my duties was to take our youngest son to his

weekly, forty-five minute cello lessons. We lived in Buitenveldert at the time and the music school was in Bachstraat in Amsterdam South. I would sometimes do some shopping while he was busy with his lesson since it wasn't quite worth going home and coming back. I also paid a visit to Rosa every now and then, a friend of my mother-in-law who had already been part of my parents' circle of friends before the war.

We still lived on Willemsparkweg and it must have been my first introduction to the idea of vegetarianism when Rosa arrived one day for a visit with her husband. My mother had bought nuts and had explained that he was a vegetarian and was accustomed to eating a lot of them. Rosa and her then husband had no children. They kept in touch with my parents, but only on occasion, and for the most part unbeknown to me.

My mother kept in touch with Rosa herself on a more regular basis. Among other things, she organised a place to stay for Max, Rosa's then boyfriend and later husband, who had run into difficulties as a result of his divorce from his second wife. Max's first wife had immigrated to Israel with two nieces who seemed to have lost their parents after the war. She and Max had raised them as if they were their own.

Rosa had returned from Bergen-Belsen after the war, but without her husband who had died two months before the camp was liberated. She once told me that when she left Holland's Westerbork transit camp she had sung 'I Love Holland' and that she had crawled into a corner of the cattle-truck in which they had been squeezed together for days on end on their way east and fallen asleep, ignoring everyone and everything around her. It seemed incredible to me, but her completely introvert personality must have come in useful in the camp.

I spent the duration of my son's cello lessons with Rosa, almost every week at one point. Max, her second husband, had passed away by this time. Our relationship became more and more intense and I grew very fond of her. She was wise in judgement, always listened attentively to whatever I had to say and never forgot to return to the subject the next time we met. Our conversations were deep and confidential and we trusted one another not to mention their content to others. Her vanity was something I actually enjoyed, especially given her age. The same vanity became extremely irritating when our friendship came to an end, but in those days she could do nothing wrong as far as I was concerned.

Rosa was the one who had advised me not to spend all my time making sure the others in my family had it their way. I liked being surrounded by cheerful faces and didn't consider it a sacrifice to have to spend most of our holidays and every summer weekend on the water. After we bought our first car, we used to drive to the sun on vacation. But Ruud, who had seen a great deal of the world on his many business excursions, took more pleasure in his boat and his sailing trips during the summer holidays.

Rosa didn't understand how I could be so docile. When I once told her my definition of sailing – taking a cold shower with your clothes on while tearing up banknotes – she didn't appreciate the joke. 'You should be more assertive,' she said. 'Those art treasures on Mrs s'Jacob's slides are real, you know! Why don't you suggest a tour, for once, by car?'

Our summer holidays were a little longer in those days, and some of them were indeed spent in the car, on Rosa's insistence, first with the children, who needed to know that there was more to the world than water, and later alone with Ruud.

When my son Job went to secondary school, he decided the time had come to cycle to his cello lessons. I thought it was dangerous with one hand on the handlebars and the other holding the cello, but the idea of being driven everywhere by his mother embarrassed him and he insisted he was no longer a child. It all had its roots in the fact that I had suggested the cello when the music school advised him to take up a stringed instrument and we had to choose between cello and violin.

Although he no longer needed my services as chauffeur, I kept up my weekly visits to Rosa, partly because the infirmities of old age prevented her from leaving the house. It became something of an obligation, a duty I didn't want to neglect. There were times it was difficult to find a spare hour, especially after I had started my career as a bookbinder and was determined to catch up on all things cultural. Now that my children were a little older, I finally had the time to get involved in the things I had been deprived of for so many years.

I enjoyed listening to Rosa's stories. She was the last of her generation to be able to talk to me about the old days. She also knew Otto and Edith Frank, having given Dutch classes to Jewish refugees from Germany in the 1930s, among them Edith Frank and Mr and Mrs Goslar, Hannah's parents.

Otto Frank had worked in the Netherlands in the 1920s, already spoke reasonable Dutch and didn't attend Rosa's classes. He came from a banker's family in Frankfurt and was charged with the opening of a branch in Amsterdam in 1923 as a result of the financial crisis in Germany at the time. But it didn't take long before the bank – M. Frank & Sons – in Amsterdam went bankrupt and Otto returned to Frankfurt in 1925. In that same year he married Edith Holländer, the daughter of an industrialist from Aachen.

Rosa told me that Edith Frank didn't attend her classes for long. She didn't feel at home in Amsterdam. The flat where they lived on the Merwedeplein was small in comparison with the mansion the family had owned in Frankfurt. She continued to miss the comfortable life they had enjoyed there with their large family and wide circle of friends. As a result, her motivation to learn Dutch wasn't strong enough. I once heard Hannah compare her own mother with Anne's mother: the intellectual and the housewife. She also compared both their fathers: Otto Frank was the salesman.

Rosa once told me a curious, confidential story about Hannah's parents. They had invited her to dinner, but her husband, a tailor who later died in the camps, didn't enjoy everyone's respect and was not invited. Hannah's father had worked for the German government as assistant minister or something like that. It didn't surprise me that he had a good rapport with the intelligent Rosa, who accepted the invitation and went alone. She told me reluctantly that she had never forgiven herself, especially in light of what was to happen.

She had already told me about the classes she had given to German Jews in the 1930s when we later met on a regular basis at Ruud's mother's house. She knew that Anne had been my friend at the Jewish school and that I had also known Hannah and her parents. She had already told me by that time that Anne's mother didn't attend the classes for long.

Anne was rarely mentioned in conversation between Rosa and Ruud's mother, and Otto Frank tended to be spoken of disapprovingly: 'All that effort to publish his daughter's book, ridiculous. Anyone could have written it.' Later, when the book had started to cause more of a furore: 'So much attention for just one child when so many people died, didn't amount to much. And Otto included himself in the limelight a little too often.'

I said nothing, unable to reply to their comments and not considering myself much of a match for both ladies together. But I found their reasoning spiteful, although the value of the book also escaped me at the time. I knew that Rosa had received a copy of the diary from Otto. In those days, the few people who had returned from the camps sought each other out, not only because they couldn't tell their story elsewhere, but also to find out if they had seen other family members in the camp.

Anne never entered the conversation during my visits to Rosa. I would tell her if there had been a gathering at the Anne Frank House, or about Otto if we had been to Switzerland, but only in passing, as part of other holiday stories. My reticence on the matter also had to do with her disapproving stance. But I could never have suspected that the distance that was later to evolve between us would have anything to do with Anne.

V

In the spring of 1986, the Dutch women's weekly *Libelle* asked for an interview about Anne, which they planned to publish in May of the same year on the occasion of the commemoration of the liberation of the Netherlands. I hesitated. The authenticated edition of the diary, a publication of the Netherlands Institute for War Documentation, in which I was to be named, had not yet appeared and, as I thought in those days, wasn't likely to attract anything close to the readership of *Libelle*. But I considered the possibility that it may have been a good opportunity to say something about the number of people who had claimed to have known Anne over the years, claims I knew to be untrue. At the beginning, when *De Achterhuis* was still selling poorly, no one was particularly interested in being Anne's 'girlfriend' or 'school pal'. I asked *Libelle* to use the name Jopie instead of my real name. It later transpired that the publishers intended to include a recent photo with the article, something I hadn't bargained for. But by then it was too late.

To my surprise, and perhaps twenty years after the war, one of the first people to use the intimate expression 'our friend Anne' in conversation with me and in the presence of others was Jenny, the girl who had stayed with us for a period of time when she returned from the camp. I was quite certain that she had not known Anne personally, and couldn't possibly have met her when Anne and I kept company because she was not living in Amsterdam at the time. Other acquaintances likewise spoke of their friendship with Anne. I didn't understand. I was prepared initially to debate the matter or explain that it didn't square with reality, but after a while I said nothing more about it. As was the case with Jenny, partners and friends were sometimes present and I didn't want to make them appear to be liars in such company. But it continued to disturb me nevertheless, and it surprised me that both men and women appeared to derive a sense of personal status from claiming to have been Anne's friend.

A boy who had been in our class at the Jewish Lyceum and had later gone into hiding also had problems with Anne's supposed friends. He didn't remember me when a second cousin of mine told him that he and I had been in the same class as Anne. He was the boy Anne had told 'the facts of life'. I knew exactly who he was when his name was mentioned. He only believed me when I reminded him that he had sat in class next to a boy called Leo. I even surprised myself that I could remember such details after twenty-five years.

I also didn't discuss the matter with my mother when I discovered that she had mentioned in an interview that she remembered more about her daughter's relationship with Anne than her daughter did. Ruud and I weren't at home the evening the interviewer arrived at the door unannounced around nine and found my mother babysitting. He was putting together a book of interviews with people who had known Anne and my mother had told him that his questions were just as welcome with her. A couple of months later I read anecdote after anecdote told by my mother and now published in book form. She had never really bothered much with my friends and I rarely spoke about them because of her apparent lack of interest. I knew that Anne had written about me in the grey cash registers in which she had continued her diary after the first book was full, the cash registers Otto had brought to our house after the war. My mother had thus been able to read about my friendship with Anne and had drawn her own conclusions. I didn't want to read Anne's writings at the time and I had still to learn that they contained descriptions of her 'passionate' gestures of friendship, but I presumed that this was what my mother was referring to when she spoke of the 'loving couple' in the interview. I was bitterly embarrassed, especially when I realised that Otto Frank would also have access to the book. Her accounts were peppered with fantasy. She had sensed to perfection what people wanted to hear about Anne and she praised her qualities to such an extent that those of her own daughters paled in comparison, especially mine.

I had often heard my mother recount a much embellished version of the anecdote about the seamstress that had been included in the interview, even in the presence of Otto and Fritzi. Anne had shown my mother her dress because she knew that she was interested in that sort of thing. She had just come back from the seamstress and I can see Anne in our living room proudly showing off her new blue dress. What the account doesn't mention is the fact that she wanted to show us how ingeniously and invisibly the dress had been lengthened. I read in the interview that my mother claimed to have sewn the dress, but this was not true.

I said nothing about the interview and kept my opinions to myself when I read it. But the admiration I had always had for my mother disappeared. She had fallen from her pedestal. Her consistently frank judgement, to which I had always attached enormous value when I was making a decision, now meant nothing to me.

I recognised the phenomenon. I drew a parallel with her own relationship with her father, whom she had always admired and respected, up to the point at least when she discovered he had been unfaithful to her mother. It inspired her to refuse to comply with his wish that his eldest daughter complete her studies. She went her own way after the discovery and started a career in the world of haute couture in Paris against her father's will. It was there that she met my father and ended up in the Netherlands.

It was to take a long time, several years after her death in fact, before I was able to appreciate my mother's qualities again for what they were.

The article in *Libelle* didn't cause much of a commotion at first. Acquaintances who were readers of the weekly and who recognised my photograph now knew that I had been Anne's friend. Some called me or spoke to me about it when we met. Others remained discreetly silent about it, having understood that I preferred not to talk about it. But this situation was soon to change.

In the spring of 1986, I saw a photo of Eva Schloss-Geiringer in *Het Parool*, one of Amsterdam's dailies, and read the accompanying article with mounting astonishment: Eva Schloss, 'childhood chum of Anne Frank', had opened the exhibition *The World of Anne Frank* in London. The paper added that she represented 'the real world of Anne Frank'. I thought for a moment that the journalist might have made a mistake, but the exhibition programme – from the Anne Frank Foundation *nota bene* – also referred to her as Anne's 'childhood chum'.

I didn't know what to make of it. I had only recently met Eva for the first time and was sure we hadn't known each other during the war. When Otto Frank brought Fritzi Geiringer – Eva's mother – over to our house for a visit, all we were told was that she had a daughter and that Heinz, Eva's late brother who had been a couple years older, had attended the Jewish Lyceum, a school system that prepared pupils for university and was divided into a 'gymnasium' section majoring in Greek and Latin and an 'HBS' section majoring in mathematics. Margot had attended the latter.

Otto Frank was doing his best in those days to trace the children who had known Anne and Margot in an effort to learn everything he possibly could about their short lives. He told me about his conversations, but Eva Geiringer was never mentioned. I would have been extremely surprised if she had, just as surprised as I now was by the article in *Het Parool*. I had learned in the meantime that the Geiringer family had lived on the opposite side of the Merwedeplein, but Eva had never been part of Anne's circle of friends. Eva's family had made the journey from Belgium to Amsterdam in 1940. She didn't attend the Montessori school with Anne, but went rather to a school in Jekerstraat. It was also evident from conversations with Otto Frank at our house shortly after the war that the Geiringer family had never made the acquaintance of the Frank family in the two years they had lived on the Merwedeplein. The other German families had lived in the neighbourhood for years and formed a relatively close group. I knew them because Anne used to take me with her for an occasional visit. There could be little doubt that something was amiss.

It was to take several years before I heard Mrs Fritzi Frank remark with regret, and on more than one occasion, that Eva had been held back a year at primary school – apparently the transition from the French-speaking Belgian school she had attended until the summer holidays of 1940 had been a difficult one – and that she had not as a result been in Anne's year at the Jewish Lyceum. She added that Eva had played with a different group of girls who were less adult than the group that surrounded Anne.

I was surprised to hear our group of friends described as 'adult'. We were just ordinary children, some twelve, others thirteen. Perhaps she was referring to the fact that Anne had been forced to grow up so quickly when she was in hiding. Anne had been surrounded by adults in the annexe and she read a great deal. As far as I was concerned this was plain to see in her writings. I myself had never met Eva or her brother during the war, although I was constantly in Anne's company on and around the Merwedeplein and I knew all of her friends and acquaintances.

But I spoke to no one about what I had read in the paper and the exhibition programme. There had to have been some kind of mistake, I thought naively, and for that reason I never mentioned it to Fritzi Frank. It was too delicate a subject. But my eyes were soon to be opened.

The article in *Libelle* inspired one of television presenter Sonja Barend's colleagues to contact me. He informed me that *The Diary of Anne Frank* – the title given to the authenticated edition put together by RIOD – was to feature in one of her programmes. They had traced me through *Libelle*. Talking live on television about Anne was the last thing I wanted to do and I refused, but when he added that Fritzi Frank and another friend of Anne, Eva Schloss-Geiringer, were also scheduled to speak, I said impulsively: 'Eva Schloss and Anne Frank were never friends.' This was reason enough to change my mind and I accepted the invitation to appear on the programme. My only condition was that I preferred not to speak about this supposed friendship on television. At the start of the programme, Sonja Barend announced that 'two friends of Anne Frank' were to appear on the show, but I knew that it would be impossible to raise the question of friendship on television without causing a major commotion.

I was taken aback for a moment when I heard that Sonja Barend planned to read passages from the diary in which Anne wrote about intimate matters between the two of us and which everyone could now read in the new edition. Her questions focused on the said passages. I made no effort to hide how much it appalled me and this resulted in a degree of hilarity. It was the first time I had appeared live on television, but the end result was positive. My unorthodox manner and evident lack of prior media training seemed to go down quite well. Fritzi talked about the goals of the Anne Frank Fund and Eva Schloss uttered a few generalities about Anne that anyone could easily have gleaned from her writings. It was clear that she had done this sort of thing before.

I now realised that Eva must have been playing this game for some time and that her mother was part of the deal, but at the time I had no idea what to do about it.

This was the second time I had met Eva. A short time before the publication of the article in *Het Parool*, I had made her acquaintance at her home in London – where Fritzi was staying – when Ruud and I happened to be on a short holiday. I had told Fritzi we were planning to be in London and she suggested we meet up at Eva's house so that she could introduce us to her daughter. Eva invited us for dinner, but we had problems on the way and arrived hours late after driving around in search of a garage to have our smashed windscreen repaired. We did our best to call her – she lived a distance outside the centre and we ended up taking the tube – but her phone was constantly busy. Eva's daughter had spent the entire time chatting with a friend. Fritzi was happy to see us. Eva made nothing of our late arrival and after dinner she showed us round her shop full of nostalgic knick-knacks.

I had a hard time being neutral towards Eva when we appeared together on Sonja Barend's television show. I also avoided the topic of Eva's supposed friendship with Anne when I spoke to Fritzi, determined as I was not to get involved.

But I couldn't help wondering what Hannah thought about the entire affair so I decided to write her a letter and ask if she remembered Eva Geiringer from the Merwedeplein. Hannah had lived there since her childhood after all and had only later moved round the corner to Rooseveltlaan or what used to be called Zuider Amstellaan. She played with Anne a lot in those days. Their parents were friends, and she and Anne had attended the same Montessori school together. I visited Hannah in hospital shortly after the war, where she was recovering from a serious illness she had contracted in the concentration camp. After that she immigrated to Israel. I met her again forty years later when she was in the Netherlands for Willy Lindwer's documentary *The Last Seven Months of Anne Frank*. The documentary focused on the last seven months of Anne's life, the months she herself would have been unable to write about, and introduced the testimony of six different women who had had contact with her in the concentration camp.

Hannah wrote back, informing me that she too had no

recollection of Eva from the Merwedeplein days, although she was otherwise pretty matter-of-fact about it. 'Anne will be laughing up there in heaven at all those "new friends" she never knew,' she wrote. I was disappointed that she had made so little of it, that she hadn't been as outraged by the affair as I had been. I had presumed that she would become an ally and offer advice on the stance we should adopt and on how to proceed. But I could only conclude that her friendship with Fritzi and Eva meant more to her than her friendship with Anne. I also realised that she had probably been aware of what had been going on for some time.

Later, when Eva Schloss published a book on her experiences in the camp and went into considerable detail about her alleged friendship with Anne, I learned that Hannah was convinced that there could never be enough books written about the Holocaust. I disagreed. As far as I was concerned, one book too many had been written, and lying about the Holocaust wasn't going to help convince those who doubted it. I couldn't stop myself from gathering evidence in support of my position, not to reinforce it in my own mind, but to prepare for the steps I knew I would have to take one day if I wanted to remain faithful to Anne's memory. She didn't deserve to have her name misused posthumously by so-called friends.

I started with Joke Kniesmeyer. She had worked at the Anne Frank Foundation for years and had been a close friend and confidant of Otto Frank. I respected her enormously. I met her at a party given by Willy Lindwer when his documentary received an Emmy Award. Eva's book, in the meantime, ghostwritten by a journalist, had been published in England, introduced onto the market with slogans like 'friend of Anne Frank' and 'Anne Frank's stepsister'. Joke told me that she was also aware that Anne and Eva Geiringer had never met.

I felt reassured: the Anne Frank Foundation were aware of the situation and would take care of it. A girlfriend more or less made no difference to them, I still thought.

Eva's Story appeared in Dutch translation in 1989 and was presented to the public at the Anne Frank House. I had already read a great deal about it in the weeklies and I obviously had my reservations. But I had always distanced myself from everything surrounding the myth of Anne Frank and I wanted to keep it that way. If I came forward as her friend to complain about the abuse of her memory, the commotion would inevitably lead to the loss of my relative anonymity. So I did my best to give her a friendly nod when she took to the platform and read a segment of her book. Children asked questions they had prepared at school. Fritzi had called me a couple of days before the event and made sure I was invited. During the telephone conversation she told me that Eva was scheduled to appear in a church in New York on 12 June to speak at a commemoration ceremony on the occasion of what would have been Anne's sixtieth birthday. I read later in American publications that Eva Schloss-Geiringer had appeared in America yet again as Anne Frank's personal friend. The authenticated RIOD edition had been published in translation by that time, together with the American edition of Eva's book. The presentation and promotion of both volumes was scheduled to take place in the presence of Eva Schloss at the opening of the *Anne Frank in the World* exhibition, likewise in New York.

My eldest son was working in New York in those days at the American branch of his Amsterdam legal firm. That afternoon I spoke to David Barnouw, one of the editors of the RIOD edition, and asked him if my son could have an invitation to the event. He said he would take care of it. I secretly hoped that I too would receive an invitation, but it never came.

My son and his girlfriend were in the church for the ceremony and reported back on every detail. His girlfriend even collected the publications related to the event and sent them to me. My anger and indignation grew as I read them, especially an evaluation of Eva's book by Rabbi Abraham Cooper of the Wiesenthal Center in Los Angeles, cited in *Legacy*, the bulletin of the Anne Frank Center in New York: "A brutally honest testimony to the truth."

'*Brutal* is the only appropriate word,' a much trusted friend remarked after reading the article.

But I was still not ready to do anything about the situation. I took the opportunity to speak to Miep Gies about it when we chatted briefly after Eva's presentation. I said nothing about the content of the book – I hadn't read it at that stage – but I didn't hide my disappointment that I had not been invited to the commemoration in New York, in spite of the fact that I had cooperated extensively on the authenticated RIOD edition that the organisers planned to promote in her presence. I had helped them trace classmates who had survived the war and were now dotted across the globe and I had made documents of my own available to them for analysis.

Miep's response was clear: 'You should have been there, not Eva.' She walked away and came back with Cor Suijk, a Foundation co-worker who organised Anne Frank exhibitions in America, and introduced us. 'I didn't know you were interested,' he said, referring to the opening of the New

York exhibition. It may have been true, but no one had ever asked me.

I read Eva's book. It was her life story, centred around the war, before, during and after. Her stories about life in Amsterdam were brimful of references to Anne and she never missed an opportunity to draw attention to the friendly relationship she had enjoyed with her and her circle of friends. I also read in the book that Heinz Geiringer, Eva's brother, had apparently been friends with Margot and that they had done their homework together. This was news to me. I knew that he had followed the senior secondary programme at the Lyceum, but was certain that Margot had not. I decided to ask Jetteke, Margot's best friend, with whom she had had daily contact, as I had had with Anne. She told me that Heinz had not been in their class, that she had never heard of he and Margot doing homework together, that he wasn't part of their circle of friends and that she had no memory of him. In Jetteke's own words: 'I know absolutely nothing of any friendship between him and Margot. If they had been friends, I'm sure Otto Frank would have said something about it when we met after the war. It's hard to imagine that he wouldn't have mentioned the coincidence when he introduced us to his second wife.' Together with Hannah's letter, this was the second piece of evidence in support of my conviction that Eva and Anne had never met. The most important piece of written evidence, however, was to be a statement from Fritzi Frank herself, handed to me ten years later. But at that moment I felt I had gathered enough information to support my position.

I thought carefully about what I should do next. I was reluctant to make too much of a scene, but I still felt obliged to object. I didn't want to tarnish the name of the Foundation, which was apparently happy to have had Eva Schloss open exhibitions as Anne's 'friend', nor did I want to tarnish Anne's own name by starting an ugly squabble about an alleged friendship.

No personal harm would come to me if I calmly let things run their course. On the contrary, if I went public I was certain to attract the resentment of others. Some might even consider it a violation of Eva's Holocaust story.

Whatever reason Eva Schloss used to justify setting herself up as Anne Frank's friend – her dreadful experiences in Auschwitz no doubt, which she was perhaps hoping to cope with via Anne, her potential greed, her probable desire for fame, or a combination of things, either conscious or unconscious – it didn't square with the truth and was thus reprehensible. I imagine some will have found her stance understandable from the psychological point of view and perhaps even justifiable, but for me it lacked decency and was plainly unacceptable. As for the Anne Frank Foundation, their position was unacceptable for historical reasons *and* reasons of decency.

I talked the matter over with friends and acquaintances but that was as far as it went. Some even wondered why it bothered me so much. I found it difficult to understand that what for me had become such an important matter of conscience could leave them so indifferent. I decided to stop talking about it. And one good friendship had already been broken because of it, with my mother-in-law's childhood friend Rosa.

But the words I had been waiting for arrived nevertheless. 'Have they lost their minds at the Foundation? You should go to them this instant and tell them you're going to do something about it if they don't,' a friend exclaimed. The intensity of her reaction took me unawares.

I thought about Anne. She would have had the same reaction. She wouldn't have laughed it off, as Hannah had suggested. She would have been just as indignant as I was. But she would have acted immediately. Floor's words made me realise there was no going back.

I wrote a letter to the governors of the Foundation, quoting passages from Eva's book that I believed to have been made up and providing appropriate comment. I explained that they were in a position to quietly ensure that Eva drop the contested passages from her book and prevent her from making further appearances as Anne's friend.

PART TWO

TROUBLE IN PARIS

1

A chronicle that covers more than a hundred years has to have its share of deaths, and it's certainly human to presume that the principle characters, who were around at the beginning, are no longer with us.

But my mother was still alive. She was already in her late nineties when my sister and I visited her in the summer of 1990 to tell her that Jeanne had passed away the previous day. My sister had received a message from Paris that morning, from the neighbour of Marie, Jeanne's sister.

My mother looked up for a moment and said: 'Order the biggest wreath you can find, in my name.' And she let it pass.

Jeanne was a few years younger than her sister-in-law, but she had also reached a respectable age when she died. She had spent the previous six months with her older sister Marie, the only surviving sister of five who lived in Paris. Although Jeanne's health was still relatively good, her hermit's existence had begun to weigh on her. The pain in her legs had worsened over the years and she was more or less housebound. Friends had advised her to move in to the new old people's home in the village, but she wasn't of a mind to do so. She was afraid of being patronised and didn't want to have to dip into her fortune. My sister telephoned Jeanne on a regular basis and I visited her once while she was with Marie. Jeanne told me that her sister quarrelled a lot and spoke about the nurse who took care of her ninety-seven-year-old sister's daily needs.

'She's after my money,' Jeanne said repeatedly, 'I don't trust her.'

My sister had been on the phone to her only three days before it happened. Jeanne had told her indignantly that the nurse had asked the week before if she could buy her earrings, the ones with the cut diamonds Albert had given her that were worth a small fortune. She had worn the earrings constantly since the day she moved in with Marie and she wanted to be buried with them. She reminded us about it often enough. The nurse's request had thrown her off balance and she was thinking about going back to the village.

When I got home from visiting my mother, I went upstairs to my workshop to think over the conversation my sister had had with Marie's neighbour. The neighbour had been very friendly, but there was something about the conversation that bothered me. When she said that Jeanne had passed away, my sister had announced that we would come immediately and arrange her affairs. But the neighbour had informed her that it wasn't necessary. Everything was going to be taken care of and all we had to do was call the next day for further details. Although I would rather have left matters to my sister, I decided to contact the neighbour myself the following day.

I walked out onto my workshop balcony and leaned over the balustrade. I could see the canals that surrounded our house, the green treetops mirrored in the water. When the trees were bare in the winter you could see the typical Amsterdam façades through the branches. My rooftop workshop offered panoramic views of old Amsterdam, illuminated exquisitely by the midday sun. In the distance, the Westerkerk tower stuck out high above the houses. Anne had lived in its shadow for more than two years in the

Achterhuis, and must have heard its bells chime on countless occasions. The sight of the tower suddenly gave me an idea.

I went inside and took down the framed drawing I had made years ago, just after the war, when I had returned for the first time to the village in France, a sketch of the Eiffel Tower from the terrace of the house with the fields in the foreground. I hammered a nail into the window frame and hung up the sketch. My painter's easel was stashed away in the corner of the room and I rarely made any use of it. But I decided there and then to dust it off and position it in such a way that I could see the Eiffel Tower and the tower of the Westerkerk side by side. I stretched a piece of canvas over a frame and mixed paint in the yoghurt pots I had rinsed out and saved in enormous quantities for the various different glues and other products I needed for my bookbinding work. I started to paint and kept going until my husband arrived home and announced that he was hungry.

I found it hard to sleep on the night train to Paris and spent the entire time fretting about one thing: why hadn't I reacted to what Marie's neighbour had said when I called her the following day. Was it just laziness on my part, and did my laziness mean that Jeanne would not be buried in the village beside her beloved Albert as she had wanted?

During the telephone conversation I was informed that we were to report to the cemetery in the district of Paris where Marie lived. The hearse with Jeanne's remains was expected there at ten o'clock. I didn't understand any of it. I was overwhelmed by the torrent of French words and didn't try to interrupt. I said we would be there, but also asked where they would be leaving from and if it was still possible to see Jeanne for a last time. It was too late, she replied, and we might as well go straight to the cemetery. I wasn't particularly keen on the idea of taking a final look at Jeanne in her coffin; I just wanted to be sure that she was wearing her earrings as she had so often insisted.

Jeanne had had the family grave in the village cemetery tidied up when Albert was laid to rest beside his parents a good twenty years earlier. She had even commissioned a magnificent marble gravestone with Albert's name and the names of his mother and father.

Every time I visited Jeanne, we would always make a point of visiting the cemetery. I would lay flowers on the grave and Jeanne would tend to the plants. On the way back she would say: 'You'll take good care of it when I'm gone, won't you.' I promised every time. Jeanne also said on one occasion: 'There's still room for your mother and for me.'

I didn't tell her that my mother had no plans to be buried in France. On the contrary, she had grown so attached to her new fatherland that she wanted to be buried in the Netherlands. Her disappointment at Albert's attitude towards her also had a part to play. She had never returned to the village after his funeral and her feelings towards her sister-in-law, who was living for free in *her* house without making the least effort to take care of it, and holding on to the money that belonged to *her* family, had grown more and more negative. Jeanne was completely unaware of my mother's reasons for staying away and she simply continued the lifestyle she had had with Albert without giving it further thought. She always seemed to be genuinely interested when she asked about Eline, my mother, and never forgot to send her best regards when I returned home. My mother received them invariably with a puff and a shrug of the shoulders.

I now came to the conclusion that we had presumed that Marie was also aware of her sister's desire to be buried in the village when we first heard news of her death. I took it for granted in fact that Jeanne had added her wish as a codicil to her will, which she kept safe in her handbag together with her other important papers and to which she had added a written reference to the earrings. I didn't want to discuss the codicil with Marie's neighbour because it included Jeanne's last will and testament and I was convinced it was none of her business.

I was confident nevertheless that Jeanne had known what had to be done, that she had remembered Albert's wishes and hadn't backed out of her obligations. A year before her death, she had invited my sister and me to come for a visit and there was a degree of urgency in the invitation. She had asked us expressly to write our names and addresses on a piece of paper together with our dates of birth and make sure there were no mistakes. The piece of paper disappeared into her handbag. I visited her again a couple of months later, before she moved to her sister's house in the city. Jeanne returned to the subject one last time, patting her handbag and telling me that she had made a *testament holographique*, which wasn't unusual in France. Why give money to a notary when a handwritten declaration had the same legal value? She said that she had had to take measures because we weren't automatic beneficiaries, unlike her sister Marie, her only surviving family member, if she outlived her of course. Nothing more was said about it after that.

We arrived at the Gare du Nord in Paris at seven in the morning and had breakfast in one of the cafés facing the station: croissants, baguettes and a couple of extra cups of coffee to make sure we were awake. We hailed a taxi and made our way to the cemetery as we had been told. I looked at my watch. It was nine o'clock. There was a florist opposite the cemetery and we bought two bouquets: one from my sister and myself, and a second from my mother, ignoring her remark that it should be bigger than the rest. We felt it would be too ostentatious, as if she had already taken advance payment on the inheritance.

We crossed to the cemetery and sat down to wait on a bench near the entrance, the bouquets between us. At ten o'clock sharp three cars arrived and we followed them to the graveside. A polished oak coffin with handsome brass fittings was removed from the first of the cars. Jeanne's elderly sister, who was more or less bedridden as far as I knew, was sitting in the second car. Marie's nurse and her husband helped her from the car. I had never met the nurse. Her husband was Marie's physiotherapist. He had introduced himself to me when we met at the door the last time I visited Jeanne at her sister's house. He had told me then in no uncertain terms that Jeanne was particularly difficult, especially towards his wife, and that she made her sister's life a misery. He and his wife now ignored us completely.

The neighbour, a woman I had never met before who was with her husband in the third car, rushed towards us, introduced herself and said solemnly: *'Permetter-moi de vous embrasser.'* We had no objection and we took the opportunity to ask her about the cause of Jeanne's sudden death.

She told us what she knew. She had found her dead in bed that morning. The doctor had been with her the day before, she said, because Jeanne had complained that the pain in her legs when she walked was getting worse. The doctor had advised her to keep taking the painkillers and suggested she use her walking stick more often. She told us Jeanne had mentioned the doctor's visit when she had popped in later that day. But as far as the doctor was concerned Jeanne was in reasonable health for her age and her neighbour had congratulated her on it.

'But what then was the cause of death?' I asked.

'The doctor diagnosed cardiac arrest,' she said, changing the subject slightly by informing me that she had bought the most beautiful coffin she could find. There had been more than enough in Jeanne's deposit account. She had summoned the nurse immediately, who had asked her that same afternoon to organise the funeral on Marie's behalf.

Jeanne, who wanted to have as little to do with banks as she did notaries, had always used her deposit account for everyday expenses because it allowed her to keep track. She didn't trust any institution that might try to pull the wool over her eyes as a well-to-do old lady. She found it bad enough that she had to delegate someone to keep an eye on her affairs, which she also administered to the best of her ability. She kept her bank book in her handbag with her other important papers. It was always stuffed with banknotes.

I took it for granted that they had also found the codicil in her handbag, but had found nothing about her desire to be buried in the village and that she had asked us to take care of it. We were also at a loss as to what to do next. Marie, who was very elderly, was whisked away by her caregivers and we didn't get the chance to ask her. She seemed confused and looked craggy and fragile.

Jeanne was buried and we laid the flowers on the grave. We offered our condolences to Marie afterwards and shook hands with the nurse and her husband, who hadn't budged from her side from the moment they arrived. We also asked the nurse if she knew what had caused our aunt's sudden death. She didn't respond directly to our question. She thought it strange that she had never seen us in Paris. 'You rarely visited Paris,' she presumed, 'and now you go to all this trouble for the funeral.' We didn't respond to her remark. I asked her a second time about the cause of Jeanne's sudden death.

'She had the same symptoms as another woman I look after. She had some sort of inflammation in her mouth and it must have affected her heart.'

Everyone disappeared all of a sudden. My sister and I took a taxi back to the Gare du Nord where we caught our train to Amsterdam at three o'clock.

My husband suggested we visit the elderly lady together to try to get some more information. He didn't trust the situation. Nonsense, I thought. I didn't want to bother the ailing old woman and definitely didn't want to have anything more to do with her caregivers, who had been so hostile towards us at the funeral. I was confident the codicil would be handed over to the notary and that all would then be revealed. I hadn't managed to check if Jeanne's wish to be buried with her earrings had been respected, but I could easily make an official request to have it confirmed. As far as I was concerned, everything was under control.

Prinsengracht 263, front (left) and rear (right) of the house, 1954.

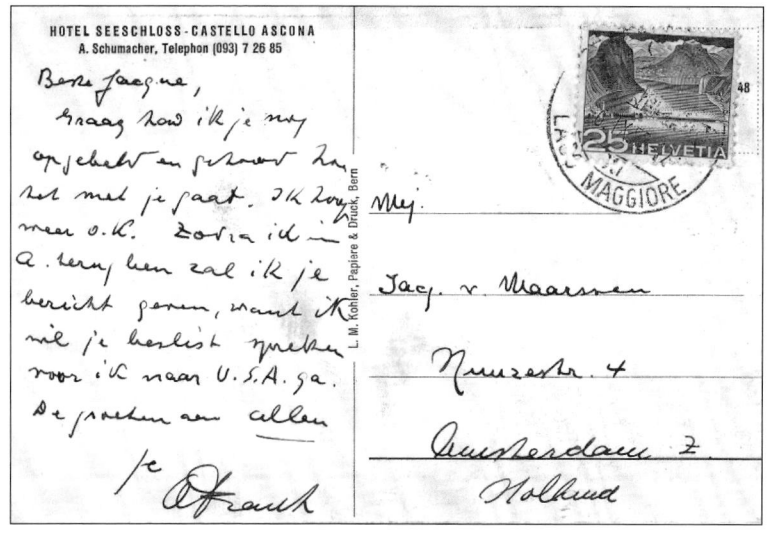

Postcard from Otto Frank to Jacqueline.

Jacqueline van Maarsen, Otto and
Fritzi Frank, 1970.

Uncle Albert.

Two sisters on a Paris terrace, 1949.

House in the village; the coffin was carried upright through the gate and into the house but had to be carried out horizontally.

My mother, circa 1970.

My sister, circa 1960.

Otto Frank, 1978.

Sailing with Ruud, 1953.

The Westertoren from the Prinsengracht, 1954.

Mother and daughter, 1973.

Jacqueline with Professor Hugo Peller in the Centro del bel Libro, Ascona, 1978.

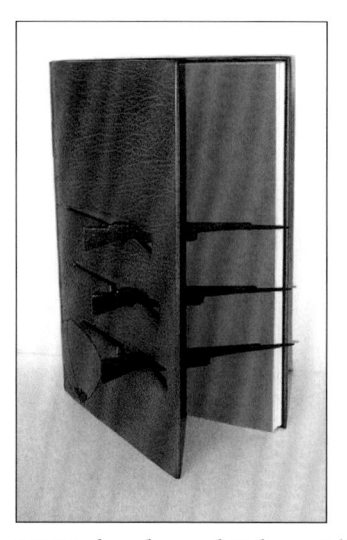

WW1 book, and Edgar Allan Poe book in black and red leather with embossed title.

Book-object, back-to-back binding.

Ruud, Jacqueline, Cor Suijk and two teachers of the Anne Frank School in Texas.

Hannah and Jacqueline, somewhat intimidated by their appearance on CNN.

Jacqueline, Ben Kingsley (Otto Frank), Hannah Taylor Gordon (Anne Frank) and Joachim Krol (Van Pels).

II

Two months passed before we heard anything further from Paris. Then we received a call from a notary's office located in the same district as Marie's home. The secretary put us through: '*Je vous passe monsieur le notaire*,' she said.

The conversation was short and to the point. The notary asked if I had keys to the house in the village. When I answered in the affirmative he asked if I would accompany him to the house so that we could go in together.

'Don't you have keys to the house?' I asked.

'No,' he replied. 'But French law prescribes that we have to enter the house together.'

That was the reason why my sister and I hadn't done so already, in spite of our curiosity.

'And did you find the codicil?'

'No, no codicil, just two beneficiaries.'

Two beneficiaries … I wondered who they might be. The notary provided the information: Marie, Jeanne's older sister, and a '*petit-neveu*' – a grandnephew. He was particularly delighted with the discovery of the second beneficiary, the work of a couple of zealous genealogists. They had dug him up somewhere in southern France and the notary referred to him from then on as 'the beneficiary'. No one, not even Marie, had ever heard of him.

The man's arrogant tone irritated me, but I made nothing of it and said: 'The codicil should have been in her handbag together with the keys.'

'I know nothing of a handbag,' he snapped, 'but we can search the house for the codicil.'

He then ended the conversation leaving me in complete bewilderment – and not for the last time.

III

The two cedars appeared left and right of the motorway, the remains of a landscape that had been forced to make way for the enormous local airport. The authorities had left them undisturbed as a living monument. Then Paris loomed in the distance, the silhouette of which had changed so much down through the years because of the high-rise buildings that I even had difficulty picking out the Eiffel Tower.

I took the ring-road and then the exit that lead to the village where I parked the car on the square and made my way to the house. I took a peek at the bistro on the way. The new proprietor was Moroccan and there was a group of young men at the bar, also Moroccan or perhaps Algerian. The bistro was an example of the changes that had taken place not far from the village.

The Parisian authorities had chosen a belt of land south of the village in the 1960s to create living space for Paris's ever expanding population. The fields disappeared under compulsory purchase, including those belonging to the father of our childhood friend Chantal. A so-called *HLM* project was set up, *Habitation à Loyer Modéré*, council houses. They had to be cheap, but the authorities did their best to make the surroundings as pleasant as possible. I checked their progress on a regular basis and they looked promising enough; plenty of space between the houses, not too much 'obligatory' green. Part of the budget had clearly been allotted to the provision of artwork on the walls and in the squares.

But it didn't take long before the project had overreached itself. Only people with the lowest incomes were given houses, many of them from former French colonies. Groups of unemployed young people hung around the streets and the graffiti on the walls became an eyesore. One of the artworks included the word *merde*. The main square was awash with litter and empty cans. The neighbourhood was going to the dogs.

When I arrived at the house, I saw three men standing at the rust-covered fence examining the ruin Jeanne had left to posterity.

I introduced myself. They were still waiting for the notary.

Two of the three men turned out to be the genealogists the notary had praised so highly over the phone and I was highly surprised to learn that the third, a man in his forties, was the alleged 'beneficiary' they had managed to dig up in the south. I decided on the spot that he wasn't getting into our house under any circumstances, but I concealed my feelings, stationed myself next to the gate and waited for the notary to put in an appearance.

One of the genealogists walked a distance up the street with the beneficiary so that they could continue their conversation undisturbed. The other started to chat with me, and I learned from our conversation the real reason why my presence was required at the opening of the house: the value of the contents had to be assessed. Without an evaluation, the beneficiaries would have to pay an extra five percent inheritance tax on the total amount, no matter what the value. I was needed because some of the furniture belonged to my mother.

I took a couple of photos of the house with its cracks and crevices, the rusty fence and the drab, crooked shutters. I was angry. Not the least because the notary had lured me to Paris under false pretences by pretending that we alone were going to search the house for the codicil. To add insult to injury, he also kept me waiting by the gate, knowing full well that I had come all the way from Amsterdam. My mood didn't improve when I noticed the *neveu* no one remembered looking the house up and down with his nose in the air. Where the man had come from all of a sudden was a mystery to me, but one thing was certain: he was from Jeanne's side of the family. The same sharp nose and the same stubborn auburn hair, short, as Jeanne used to wear it. But what struck me most was his chubby, thickset build. It was as if Jeanne had come to life again in front of my eyes.

After I had waited by the gate in the hot sun for at least half an hour, two cars turned into the street, the one after the other. A man and two women emerged from the first. One of the women was Marie's nurse. What was she doing here I asked myself. She had hitched a lift from the notary and his secretary. When it transpired that the assessor was in the other car everything became clear to me. The *neveu* had come for the evaluation – all the way from southern France – and the nurse as Marie's authorised representative. She too had to be present by law.

There I was, surrounded by seven strangers, and I was going to have to let them into our house whether I liked it or not.

The notary instructed me to open the padlock and chain but it refused to budge. No one had been inside the house for months and the padlock was rusted solid. My hands were shaking from pent-up rage and the notary had to help me with both the padlock and the gate. He then announced that he was going inside with the assessor and the secretary

– who had brought a typewriter – and that we should remain outside for the time being. I was allowed to climb the stone stairs to open the front door, and when I expressed my displeasure at not being allowed any further he turned on me: 'Do you want me to look for the codicil or don't you? French law prescribes that you are not allowed to be present for such a search and that I must go in alone.'

I was convinced that the codicil was not in the house. It was or had been in Jeanne's handbag, the handbag that was now missing. I had to accept the situation. French law was French law and there was little I could do about it. I sat down on the crumbling stone stairs and a few minutes later the typewriter started to clatter.

I looked around at the weeds that had started to take over the terrace and the garbage under the stairs: old newspapers, advertising leaflets and empty bottles that had been tossed through the fence. I felt flushed and ill at ease. The genealogists had returned to their car. After a few minutes, the nurse and the nephew appeared.

'There's nothing stopping us from sitting here, is there?' she said.

I nodded almost imperceptibly and the two sat down at the bottom of the stairs and whispered to one another in private.

After a while listening to the clatter of the typewriter, a familiar face suddenly appeared at the gate. It was Chantal's husband Alain. We had kept them posted about everything that had happened since Jeanne's death. They knew we were going to be in the village – my sister had been unable to come at the last minute – and we had to pay them a visit after we had settled our affairs at the house.

'I'm not allowed into my own house,' I said.

'Is there anything I can do?' he asked.

'Nothing, I'm afraid, it's French law apparently.'

'*Ça alors*, utter nonsense,' he said. 'Let them try and stop me!'

The nurse and the nephew listened with open ears to our conversation. I signalled to Alain that he should keep his voice down and told him who was sitting at the bottom of the stairs. I stopped him from going inside. I was determined to stay calm. Jeanne's handbag had not yet been found and I didn't want to get on the wrong side of the notary. Alain left, wished me good luck and said: 'Pop in as soon as you can.'

The chat with Alain did me the world of good. I was also happy that the two at the bottom of the stairs had witnessed the conversation. Now they knew that I had friends in the village. The nurse, who had implied at Jeanne's funeral that we never came to visit, now knew better.

The notary appeared at the door forty-five minutes later. 'You have my permission to enter the house first,' he said condescendingly. 'There was no sign of the codicil.'

As we walked into the house, I said: 'I'll have to ask my son to look into this for me. He's a lawyer.'

I immediately regretted having used my son Mark yet again to reinforce my own ego. The notary pretended not to have heard my remark and made his way into the house ahead of me. He showed me a scrap of paper he had found on the kitchen table containing the text normally used for a *testament holographique* but without any names. I noticed that the handwriting was not that of aunt Jeanne. She must have used it as an example, but the notary pointed out in no uncertain terms that the document was without value since it was undated and made no reference to specific beneficiaries.

At that point he allowed the remainder of the group into the house. The nurse was the first to enter and she looked around with curiosity. The nephew did the same, but with his nose turned up again as was apparently his wont. The genealogists didn't venture beyond the doorway.

I then discovered Jeanne's golden earrings lying on the table, hidden between the unwashed glasses, dog-eared playing cards, well-thumbed romance paperbacks, writing and sewing material, piles of papers and other more amorphous bits and bobs that covered the tablecloth. I brought them to the notary's attention. Jeanne had apparently taken off the earrings she had always worn before she left the village. The earrings I had seen her wear when she was living with Marie were the diamond ones Albert had given her.

'Take them with you,' the nurse suggested with a hypocritical grin, 'as a memento of your aunt.'

No one spoke. It wasn't the nurse's place to share out the inheritance. She said nothing more after that, but the nephew, who was particularly tight-lipped, popped the earrings in his pocket. He appeared to have little interest in aunt Jeanne's furniture, with the possible exception of the table and chairs, which were the only items he looked at in any detail. They were the only pieces of furniture in the room that had belonged to my grandparents.

'*Ajoute boucles d'oreilles*, include the earrings,' the notary muttered dryly, and the secretary typed them in at the bottom of the list.

'Gold,' the assessor added in a last attempt to boost their value and he looked at me for a second. The secretary, who was stationed in front of her typewriter docilely awaiting the orders of her boss, the notary, had difficulty containing her laughter.

As the only person present considered capable of doing so, I was asked to point out the furniture that had belonged to Jeanne: the kitchen cabinet and the wardrobe still side by side in the living room, a couple of imitation leather armchairs, and the sofa on which Jeanne had slept for years before she moved to Paris. The inheritance taxes weren't likely to amount to much.

I then made my way upstairs with the assessor to show him the hatch that lead to the attic.

'You would be forgiven for thinking that no one has been here in years,' he said as he climbed the ladder.

'Is my bike still up there?' I asked when I heard him clattering around upstairs.

'What remains of it, yes, in the corner,' he replied, 'and there's an old gramophone, some records and a zither in deplorable condition.'

'That'll be my grandfather's zither, and the records are marches by the *Garde Républicaine*. He used to be a member.' Grandfather played them for us often.

As the assessor clambered down the ladder I noticed that the smart, dark-blue suit he had been wearing was now grey with dust.

'All that junk,' he said to me. 'I feel sorry for you. There's nothing of any value up there. It's all broken and mouldering away. It's going to cost you a bob or two to get rid of it.'

I spoke to the notary about it. 'I'll send you a bill for the removal of the furniture I pointed out to you,' I said.

'What's the point?' he replied, 'they might as well go with the rest.' Without asking my opinion, he now appeared to be taking it for granted that the entire house was to be emptied. I said nothing, although I planned to write to him from Amsterdam to claim my expenses.

The notary jotted down my parents' dates of birth. He looked up for a moment when he heard my father's Jewish name. I may have imagined it, but from that moment onwards he seemed to be even less agreeable, if such were possible.

The legal declaration had been drawn up in juridical French and he read it at breakneck speed. It was hard to pay attention and I wasn't sure if I had understood it all. This man was a xenophobic anti-Semite or an anti-Semitic xenophobe, whatever you want to call it. I realised to my surprise that the sense of inferiority I always experienced when situations reminded me that I was different, that I didn't belong, had disappeared. I knew this had to do with a battle I was waging elsewhere in my life and that my resilience had grown. All these thoughts filled my mind as he read and I missed much of what he had to say as a result.

Before signing the document I took him to one side for a second. I wanted to know if I was ceding any of my rights. After all, Jeanne's handbag was still missing and there was still a chance that the codicil would be found.

'All you're signing for is the contents of the house. You can confirm it with your son, the lawyer,' he observed cleverly. He had heard my remark in the doorway after all.

The reading of the declaration finally filled in some gaps on the relationship between Jeanne and her *neveu*.

The sisters had also had a brother who died in 1918 at the age of eighteen. The notary read aloud: *Mort pour la France*, died for his country. But just before his death he had managed to get a young girl pregnant. She lived near the place where he was billeted and she gave birth to a son who was later to be the father of the *neveu*. It was clear that both families had agreed that the child be recognised and he thus acquired his natural father's name.

The *neveu* had been ignorant of the existence of his great aunts. He had travelled to Paris from his home in the south of France and had met Marie for the first time the day before. He now pointed to a framed photo of Jeanne, sitting in the sun with Toutou in her arms. I had taken the photo myself.

'Why don't you take it with you,' I said, 'she was your aunt after all.' I was angry at Jeanne. She had been foolish enough not to have a proper will made up, and all because she hated notaries. Although I shared her aversion to the full at that moment, I blamed myself for not following my husband's advice and drawing Jeanne's attention to the risks attached to a *testament holographique*. Hindsight is always twenty-twenty, of course, and fretting about the situation wasn't going to help. It was looking more and more as if we'd been taken for a ride.

IV

Once the pile of typed pages had been signed by all present, the notary and his entourage left. The house was cheerless and cold, in spite of the warm weather, and they clearly couldn't get out of it quick enough. The notary had opened the shutters and windows to let in some light. The grey and grimy net curtains fluttered in the breeze.

For the first time in my life I was alone in the house. As a child I had stayed here every year with my grandparents and later Albert and Jeanne were always here when I visited. I found an empty rubbish bag in the kitchen and opened it out on a dust covered chair before sitting down. I looked around. It seemed as if the only thing we were going to inherit from aunt Jeanne was the chaos surrounding me, and it was going to cost us money into the bargain. Piles of papers filled the gaps between the clutter on the table and the cupboards, apparently left untouched. It was obvious that the notary hadn't searched very thoroughly for the codicil. There were even unopened letters. He had fished around for documents in a couple of half-open drawers, piled them up on the table and taken them with him without further comment.

I closed the windows and shutters, left the room and made my way hesitatingly upstairs. I hadn't been in the bedrooms for years, and I knew that Jeanne had confined herself to the ground floor after Albert passed away. She would have thought this odd of me and certainly wouldn't have appreciated it.

Lying on the floor of the tiny side room where we used to sleep as children I saw a small picture frame, its glass was

broken. It was uncle Albert's *Croix de Guerre* with certificate and all. I took it out of the frame. It had been awarded to those who had served France with bravery during World War I. Although the poisonous gases used by the Germans during the war had left Albert with lung problems, the family had been particularly proud of this medal of honour.
I also found a framed photograph of my mother perched in between a Volendam fisherman and his wife. It had always been there. I took the photo from the wall. It dated from the early years, when my parents were still in the first flush of love, and there was something endearing about it.

I opened some of the drawers in my grandparents' bedroom and found a satin box containing three locks of hair, three blonde curls tied with a ribbon. I presumed they had belonged to my mother and her brother and sister. I returned them to the drawer. There was a framed photograph next to the box of a chubby little baby on a white fleece. I didn't know who the baby was, but it wasn't hard to hazard a guess. I removed the photo from the frame. 'René' was written on the back. I looked again at the handsome little lad in the photo. It was aunt Yvette's son. Plagued by her nerves, my mother's sister had jumped in the Seine with little René in her arms. They managed to rescue her but her baby was taken lifeless from the water. My mother managed to get her sister into a psychiatric institution and avoid prosecution and a prison sentence for murder.

I couldn't help thinking of the sorrow my grandmother must have felt at the loss of her grandchild, her only grandchild at the time. I knew the feeling. 'Do you still think about him so much?' Ruud asked a couple of months after I found our first son dead in his cot. 'Every minute of the day,' I had replied.

I took the photo with me. After René's drowning, my mother gave up her determination not to have any children in an effort to comfort my grandmother. My sister and I have the death of little René to thank for our own lives.

I removed a photo of my sister, taken on the beach at Zandvoort when she was about two years old, from its frame and added it to a pack of postcards with my mother in them as a young girl, printed to commemorate the great flood of Paris in 1910. I also found some letters in my mother's handwriting and stacked everything together with a few newspaper cuttings from World War I. I then opened the linen cupboard where my grandparents' black outfits were still hanging, musty and grey with dust. They wore them every Sunday to church. I quickly closed the cupboard door and hurried downstairs with my findings under my arm.

The door to the cellar was open and I made my way carefully downstairs, stopping on the last step as I had done in the past when I watched my grandfather tap wine from one of the huge vats. He once called us over to take a look. He was standing next to the wine rack that covered an entire wall and was filled with row after row of neatly stacked bottles. He singled out a number of them and let us read the labels. These were the exquisite wines, only to be opened on special occasions.

I could make out a variety of things in the semi-darkness: a wheelbarrow, with uncle Albert's gardening clogs still in it, chairs, cupboards, cardboard boxes. The wine vats were gone although the wooden trestles that had once supported them were still there. The wrought-iron wine rack was where it had always been, but now it was empty. A musty cardboard box containing wineglasses was perched on the floor beside it.

The gloomy cellar gave me the shivers so I hurried upstairs with the box of wineglasses. I was surprised to see on closer inspection that the glasses matched the glass carafe my mother always used to pour iced tea with slices of lemon during the summer. She had given it to me and I still used it for flowers.

I transferred the glasses to another box, the contents of which – Jeanne's sewing kit – I had emptied onto the table. I put all the things I had found upstairs in a plastic bag and placed the box of glasses on top. I took a last look around and retrieved Jeanne's clock from the mantelpiece. I then made my way outside with my heirlooms, locked the door behind me, crossed from the courtyard to the terrace and closed the door that separated them. I took a moment to enjoy the afternoon sun.

Jeanne's next-door neighbour was waiting behind the fence that separated his garden from the terrace. 'It's not going to be easy getting rid of decades' worth of junk,' he said. The man was no stranger to me. He used to pick up groceries for Jeanne from time to time and pass them through the gate. No one was allowed up the stone stairs. 'Here's hoping they finally do something with the house and the terrace,' he continued. He told me that he had tried often enough to persuade Jeanne to have the house whitewashed and employ a gardener. She had brushed him off with the same words for the best part of twenty years: 'It won't be long before I'm gone. It's not worth it.' She didn't pay any attention to his remark that there was every chance she would reach a hundred. A hundred years was too precise a deadline for her. But he had always been kind to her and had driven her to the doctor on occasion or to the post office when she needed to withdraw some money. I had also heard that he had brought her to her sister's house in Paris and asked if he remembered seeing her black handbag.

'Not just any old bag,' he said with a meaningful wink.

'There's no sign of it,' I said.

'I can testify to the fact that she had it with her when she went to her sister's,' he said. He remembered how she had been careful to set it next to her on the back seat of the car. It was stuffed with banknotes together with all her important papers.

I now had proof that Jeanne had taken the handbag with her when she moved in with her sister Marie and that she, as always, had never let it out of her sight.

I crossed the weed-choked terrace and descended the stone stairs. The rusty padlock on the gate refused to budge. A young black man was passing at that moment and he helped me with it. I had a mind to tell Alain about him. Alain did nothing but complain about the newcomers to the village. A bunch of scroungers living off *our* taxes, he would grunt. I hinted sometimes that it had to do with France's colonial past, but I always avoided getting into a discussion about racism and discrimination. Chantal's family knew a little about our background. They had picked up something about it during the war when Albert was trying to get hold of copies of my mother's grandparents' birth and baptismal certificates from the unoccupied part of France. They had been necessary to convince the German *Sicherheitsdienst* in Amsterdam that my mother, my sister and myself were not Jewish. Albert had wisely said nothing about the fact that he had enlisted aunt Julie and her collaborating husband to help procure the papers, but they knew about the difficulties we had been facing in Amsterdam because my father had registered us as part of the Jewish community just before the war. Beyond that, Alain and Chantal knew nothing about my life in Amsterdam, and absolutely nothing about my friendship with Anne Frank and its consequences.

'Do you have any idea how much Albert inherited back then?' Chantal's father asked later as I refreshed myself with a huge glass of fruit juice. He was a spry eighty-year-old who had moved in with his daughter and son-in-law after his wife had died.

I had never really thought about it. I left that to my mother, but even she could only have guessed. I was pretty sure though that it must have been close to a couple of hundred thousand Dutch guilders.

'Millions,' said Chantal's father. Albert had confided this to his best friend at the time and made him promise not to breathe a word.'

'Old francs I imagine,' I said. I knew the French had been juggling with figures ever since the franc had been revalued by a factor of 100.

'Six million new francs,' he said. 'And if you take their thrifty lifestyle into account they probably didn't even put a dent in it,' he added.

Alain started to think aloud.

Who stood to benefit from the disappearance of the handbag and Jeanne's will? The *neveu* knew nothing about it, and what would an old woman of ninety-seven want with all that money? She couldn't even get out of bed without the help of her caregivers. The nurse had handed over Jeanne's deposit account book to her next-door neighbour when she asked her if she would take care of the funeral arrangements. The book had always been in Jeanne's handbag, the same handbag that contained her will. Everything pointed towards one person, someone Marie depended on for everything, someone who could have persuaded her to make up a will in her favour without too much trouble.

'The nurse,' I blurted. I had also been thinking about the cause of death and the two different stories that had been dished up about it.

Had I been watching too many detective series on television?

Alain tugged on his eyelid with his index finger as if to say 'Do you get the picture?' Chantal added that she was also certain that Jeanne wanted to be buried in the village.

'*On vous a eu*, you've been diddled,' she said. But all we had were presuppositions and no hard evidence. We had to find the handbag.

Chantal's daughter-in-law Gabrielle, who had been following the conversation, turned to me out of the blue and said: 'You speak pretty good French for a Dutchwoman.'

'Makes sense,' said Alain, 'her mother's French.'

'Language is not something you inherit,' Gabrielle insisted. 'You have to speak it with your children when they're still young.'

It was the first time I'd heard such a remark in these surroundings. That's the way it is, I observed. Gabrielle had unconsciously touched on the problems I had had as a child with the French language because my mother was always away at work during the day. It was never a consideration for my mother and my French grandfather who didn't try to hide their irritation when I made a mistake.

I phoned home to bring them up to date on the day's events. Ruud had just arrived home and he told me I should get back as soon as possible. My mother, who had been suffering from a serious cold when I left for Paris, was running a fever and the doctor had diagnosed pneumonia. Given her age it was potentially fatal.

Alain promised he would find someone to buy up the contents of the house and empty it. I left early the following morning for Amsterdam and my mother. She was living in an old folk's home in those days, in Het Gooi near Hilversum, and was close to my sister who had married by that time and returned to the Netherlands from England.

V

The crisis had already passed by the time I arrived at the home. She had responded well to medication and the fever was gone. Her sturdy constitution had pulled her through once again.

But for the first time she didn't appear to recognise me. 'Oh,' she said, 'I'm so happy to see you. People have said such good things about you!'

I panicked. I put it down to the red jacket I was wearing. I never wore red. My own jacket had been covered in dust and grime from the visit to the house and I had thrown it away. The red jacket belonged to Gabrielle.

But it had nothing to do with the jacket. Her mind returned to its usual clarity after the pneumonia subsided, but as the year went on there were more and more moments like this, when she didn't recognise one of us. Her eyesight was very poor and she was virtually deaf. If my 'Mama, it's me' didn't get through to her, she would reach out and hold my hands. She recognised my hands. And she spoke only Dutch when we talked, as she used to when I was young. In those days she thought I didn't understand her when she spoke to me in French because I always answered back in Dutch. I was more worried about the criticism she would level at me if I made mistakes in French, but I understood her well enough. French was still a common feature of our day-to-day existence and we often visited my grandparents in France. As I grew up she started to speak to me in French only, but she had apparently forgotten about it.

At a given moment, in her late eighties, when she could still get around and her mind was still clear, she decided she wanted to move to a rest home. The doctor suggested the Hospice Wallon in Amsterdam, an institution founded in the seventeenth century for elderly and deprived Huguenots. The place still had a few French-speaking residents, but such a move would have been out of the question for her. The hospice's statutes had never been changed and they still insisted that only Protestants could make use of the facilities. French women with Catholic roots were not welcome.

For this reason she moved away from Amsterdam and its long rest home waiting lists. My sister had managed to find a place for her in a home near to where she lived.

At the beginning, when she still seemed immortal, she enjoyed the parties and get-togethers the home organised to the full. But she didn't mix much with the other residents. She was too much the odd one out, and besides, few of the other residents interested her. The only new friendship she established was with a woman in a neighbouring room who used to be a nurse and who spoke to her in French. The first time she gave us a tour of the place she showed us the fitness room with great pride and demonstrated each of the machines. It was the first time we had ever seen her exercise.

She had also made friends with a horse that was paddocked next door to the home. She brought it chunks of bread every day and fed it by hand. It didn't take long before the horse got to know her and came galloping over when she appeared at the fence.

She continued to stick her nose in everywhere, of course, as she had always done in the past. One day she caught sight of one of the other residents walking outside in shirtsleeves and slippers and went after him. 'What are you doing?' she asked. 'I'm going to The Hague,' he replied. 'No, not today, you have to get back inside, you can't go to The Hague,' she insisted, and when he refused she simply pulled him by the braces to the entrance of the home where the nursing personnel took over. It was hardly surprising that she quickly became something of a celebrity.

The more my mother's inability to look after herself increased, the more my sister kept a careful eye on the nurses. She regularly inspected the medication that had been prescribed for her and to help her keep track of things she volunteered to help with lunch a couple of days a week. This was much appreciated by the staff, who were even willing to put up with her bossiness. I visited my mother no more than once a week. Unlike my sister, whose activities at the home brought some relief from the monotony of everyday existence as a housewife, I found it difficult to be surrounded by so much mental and physical deterioration, of which my mother was now a part. She would tell my sister about it with elation when Ruud and I paid her a visit, but when I asked if she had seen my sister the previous day, she invariably replied: 'That one never shows her face!' I saw the funny side of the situation and told my sister about it, but she wasn't exactly amused.

In spite of everything, my account of the visit to the village seemed to reach its mark. I wisely held my tongue about the 'beneficiary', but I told her all about Jeanne's missing handbag and the nurse's strange behaviour. I expected her to be furious but all she did was nod and tell me she was tired and wanted to sleep.

PART THREE

REMEMBER EVERY LAST DETAIL

I

It took quite some time before the Anne Frank Foundation responded to my letter, but when they finally did I was far from satisfied. Because I lived in a totally different world, in which art and culture held pride of place, money played a secondary role and power was of no significance whatsoever to me. I had not realised that an entire generation had arisen in the meantime who depended on World War II for a living. Of course, I had nothing against neutral academic research or work aimed at countering prejudice, discrimination and oppression.

I always did my best to make Anne as human as possible and whittle away at the mythical aura that had been built up around her, but it was this very myth of Anne Frank that the professionals needed for their work. And when I sensed that the boundaries had been reached, they on the contrary produced their reasons to breach them. They didn't share the norms I valued so much, that had become very clear to me.

My conscience wouldn't let me leave this alone. I knew that I had to speak for Anne because she could no longer speak for herself and I decided I had to do something to put an end to the abuse of her name. I was able to count on the help of Hélène, a friend of my daughter Liane. My life was about to take a completely different turn.

'It's enough to make your hair stand on end,' Hélène Weyel had exclaimed when my daughter told her about the problems I had been having with Eva Schloss-Geiringer's book and the Anne Frank Foundation.

'She wants to do an interview with you about it for *Vrij Nederland*,' Liane informed me. 'She's already had a word with the chief editor ...'

'Joop van Tijn didn't beat about the bush,' Hélène told me later. 'Write the article!' When I spoke to him myself after the commotion could no longer be contained, he said: 'They've been fostering a viper in their midst and for one reason or another they can't back away from it.'

Hélène came to the house for preparatory discussions. I told her about my friendship with Anne. Liane had given her a copy of the article that had appeared in *Libelle* four years earlier and she had it with her.

We agreed that what I had spoken of in such guarded terms in *Libelle* should now be exposed to the full light of day. Hélène's obvious indignation encouraged me to speak freely about the way Anne Frank had been abused by Eva Schloss's book for the sake of ... that was it, for the sake of what? She seemed to understand why I had hidden behind the name Jopie up to that point and why I had now decided to go public in *Vrij Nederland*, a paper with a very different and more critical readership than *Libelle*.

I showed her video recordings of the launch of the authenticated edition of Anne Frank's diary in Amsterdam in 1986. RIOD had made the effort to track me down for their research but had apparently forgotten to invite me to the launch. I had lent them documents with Anne's handwriting that I had preserved from the war. The book even included a facsimile of a page from my poetry album, in which Anne had dedicated a poem to me.

The video contained images of Eva Schloss leafing through Anne's original diary. To my horror, she handled the little chequered book that I found so endearing as if it were a throwaway paperback. Eva presented herself once again as Anne's friend, just as she had done during the TV interview with Sonja Barend, which we had also viewed on video. I had decided not to look at it any more to spare myself further irritation, but now I thought: what possessed you to keep silent about this for all these years? But it was only after reading Eva's book that the urge to do something about it took hold of me and refused to let go. I read Hélène the letter I had sent a couple of weeks earlier to the governors of the Anne Frank Foundation. Her indignation grew with each new point it raised.

'You don't mince your words,' she said. 'It promises to be an excellent article.' She told me how surprised she was that I had yet to receive an answer from the Foundation. The answer arrived a couple of days later and Hélène came over to read it.

It only served to reinforce our decision. I was reminded of the doubt a friend had expressed when I told him a little earlier about the *Vrij Nederland* interview. 'An article in the paper is too superficial. Don't think it'll get you anywhere. You should write a book.'

'Would you like to be my ghostwriter,' I asked Hélène who had already published a number of books. 'I wouldn't mind,' she said, 'but I think you should write it yourself. I've read your letters to the Anne Frank Foundation and I think you've got it in you.'

I replied to the Foundation's letter. They had written about Eva's 'purity of motive' when she wrote her book. I focused in my reply on 'purity of content'. They had written that they had 'no reason to doubt the personal integrity of Fritzi Frank and Eva Schloss'. In response to this and to their request for a description of my own 'enormously valuable experience' as a contribution to the Anne Frank Archive administered by the Foundation, I replied: 'Why should a description of my own experience be of any value to the archive? Even after reading my letter, you still find no reason to question the integrity of Fritzi Frank and Eva Schloss. What use then would a description of my own personal experience be to your archive? I have never doubted Fritzi Frank's integrity – without evidence to the contrary. But maintaining an archive obliges you to authenticate the material you include in it.'

My letter also mentioned the remark made by Joke Kniesmeyer, a staff member at the Foundation, who had told me that she was also aware of the fact that Anne and Eva Geiringer had not known each other before. The Foundation's response was diplomatic: 'There must have been some kind of misunderstanding. She can't imagine ever having made such a remark.' I decided not to pursue the matter for Joke's sake and wrote back that she had perhaps forgotten what she had said.

I wrote in the same letter that Cor Suijk, former director of the Anne Frank Foundation and the organiser of the Foundation's exhibitions and other manifestations in the USA, had suggested that I be present at the opening of an Anne Frank exhibition in Las Vegas and be given the opportunity to tell my story. I told them I was prepared to do as he suggested.

A friend with whom I shared my experiences, the one who had remarked on the use of the word 'brutally' in the article Rabbi Abraham Cooper had published in the bulletin of New York's Anne Frank Center, compared the situation with what had happened to her father-in-law. He had played an important role in the resistance during the war, but for some reason had been kept out of the various post-war committees that had been set up to honour its fighters. He had been an eyewitness, but had later been forced to look on with regret as others received all the glory. Both instances might seem worlds apart, but it had to do with the integrity of two organisations sharing similar ethical aspirations that did not always behave in an ethical manner, organisations that feigned ignorance when people dealt dishonestly with the lives of men and women who had died or endured enormous personal danger in the resistance or the life of a young girl who passed away in a concentration camp. And all for personal status and gain.

I told my story to *Vrij Nederland* in two sessions. It made a deep impression on me, not only because I had to delve into the distant past, but also because I felt compelled to talk about the less than agreeable events that had followed. At the end of the interview, I announced my plan to put the entire affair down in writing.

In September 1989, the day after the article appeared in the paper, I received a phone call from a publisher with an offer to publish the book. I told him I still had to start writing it, but that I would contact him as soon as it was ready.

A letter to the editor was published in the next edition of *Vrij Nederland*, submitted by the Anne Frank Foundation and containing, among other things, the following: 'She [Eva Schloss] is exceptionally unassuming and reticent about her friendship with Anne.' It also quoted from a typed letter and curriculum vitae signed and submitted by Otto Frank to the Anne Frank Foundation in 1975: 'Eva, who was the same age as Anne, knew her and they played together on the square.' The Foundation sent me a copy of the letter and CV within the week. I was later informed that Otto Frank had already written in a letter from 1959 that Anne and Eva Geiringer 'frequently' played together on the square. For one reason or another, the 'frequency' of the encounters had no longer seemed important in 1975. The letter to the editor also stated that this was not the first time that I had come forward with the story of my friendship with Anne and alluded to the article in *Libelle*. The article in *Vrij Nederland* had not suggested that this was the first time I had gone public with my story, but those responsible for the paper's layout had added a headline to that effect above the text.

The first quotation with the words 'unassuming' and 'reticent' irritated me intensely. I ascribed Eva's reticence to the fact that one cannot write much about what one does not know. The second quotation amazed me. Otto had never spoken to me about Eva and Anne playing together. Where did he get this from? Her other friends never witnessed any such moments. I talked to Kitty about it, a neighbour who had also lived on the Merwedeplein and someone I knew Anne had liked. Otto and I had initially thought that Anne's diaries were addressed to Kitty, the neighbour, until I discovered that the real addressee was the girlfriend of Joop ter Heul, the main character in the books of Cissy van Marxveldt, which we loved to read so much. When I later read Anne's writings in their entirety and realised how much of the first part of her diary had been written in the style of Cissy van Marxveldt, it struck me that the diary also contained letters to the members of the Jopopinoloukiko club, the imaginary friends of Joop ter Heul from the series of the same name. It then dawned on me that Anne had addressed her diaries to Kitty from the series, Joop ter Heul's favourite girlfriend. I also realised why Anne had referred to me in the second version of her diary as Jopie, after Joop ter Heul.

I met Kitty – the neighbour – at a party given by Melissa Müller in 1998 on the publication of the Dutch translation of her biography of Anne Frank. It was the first time that we had seen each other in all those years. Melissa had interviewed several of Anne's neighbours for the book and many of them were present for the launch. Kitty made it clear to me that she also found Eva's claims a source of irritation. Melissa told me that Eva had protested about her book because it had confined her to the sidelines and had stated that she and Anne had never met.

I found it particularly distasteful that the Anne Frank Foundation had involved Otto Frank in the fray. If I had known about his letters I might not have gone public with the entire affair. I would certainly have been torn by the thought that what I was about to do ran the risk of bringing Otto Frank, who had always been very dear to me, into discredit.

I couldn't stop thinking about the situation. I was reminded of the story Fritzi always told about meeting Anne at the dressmaker's. The enormous similarity between this and the anecdote my mother regularly told about Anne returning from a visit to the dressmaker and showing my mother her recently altered dress was already obvious to me. Anne considered my mother something of an authority when it came to clothing. I now presumed that this story, which had been 'authorised' by Otto, was intended to introduce his second wife into the legend of Anne Frank. They spent many years together presenting the message contained in Anne's diary and helping to spread it across the world. I understood the fact that he had created a role for his wife as nothing more than a kind gesture.

I thought at first that she had invented it after Otto's

107

death. On further inquiry, however, RIOD produced an article taken from an English newspaper from the 1970s, published while Otto was still alive, in which Fritzi tells her dressmaker story.

Eva's book also makes reference to the story, but in her version she herself is present as well.

I asked RIOD if they had anything in their archives about the Jewish Lyceum. They said they had nothing, but they gave me the number of a woman, Xandra van Gelder, who was doing research into the history of the Lyceum. I called her and told her that RIOD had claimed to have nothing in its own archives about the Lyceum. 'Oh, is that what they said?' she responded with surprise. She told me that she had been allowed by RIOD to look through a box of papers on the Lyceum as part of her research. I was looking for class lists to help me verify the information I had on Heinz Geiringer. I still believed in those days that verifiable arguments would help put matters right. The author of *Eva's Story* had given her imagination free rein once again on the friendship between Heinz and Margot. In my letter to the Foundation, I provided the names of witnesses – among them Margot's bosom friend Jetteke – who were still alive and who would not hesitate to contradict her on the matter. I heard nothing further about it.

I gained an ally at one point, albeit from unexpected quarters, in the form of the chairperson of the Anne Frank Fund in Basel, which administered the funds that had flooded in from the sale of *The Diary of a Young Girl*. Vincent Frank-Steiner and I had met before. We understood one another, and he had enjoyed the conversations we had had about Anne. He and Otto had become good friends (although they were not family, in spite of the name) and Otto had appointed him as his successor on the Fund's board of governors, granting him a double vote when he became the board's chairman. I hadn't been planning to bother Vincent with the Eva Schloss affair, but he called me around that time to ask about a request he had received from the editors of the *Pottenagenda* – a diary for lesbians – who wanted to include the fragment from Anne's diary in which she writes about fondling breasts. I explained that 'pot' was Dutch slang for lesbian and he decided not to give permission.

I took the opportunity to tell him about the controversy I had found myself in with the Anne Frank Foundation. He seemed a little insulted about the fact that he hadn't been informed about it and that I hadn't sent him a copy of my letter to the Foundation. I was surprised that the Foundation had not briefed him on our correspondence and told him that I had been wary about getting him involved because of his friendship with Fritzi. I promised to send him a copy of my exchange of letters with the Foundation. He informed me that his relationship with Fritzi had soured a little. The Fund had subsidised the publication of Eva's book, but she had refused to pay it back when the book started to earn a profit. It had also annoyed him that Eva had referred to herself without justification as Anne Frank's stepsister when she was promoting the book, but he felt unqualified to offer judgement on the truth content of the rest of Eva's story.

I faxed him the letters and once he had read them he replied: *With reference to our shared problem: it does not surprise me in the least that the Foundation's reaction was dismissive since they cannot risk a quarrel with Fritzi. In addition, it would be too risky for the Foundation to suddenly abandon the strong ties it has established with Eva.*

You are one of the few people who has never tried to profit from Anne Frank and there is little question that you knew her extremely well, far better than many of those who are presently and unashamedly capitalising on their relationship with her.

His last remark was particularly interesting. I had been careful to avoid any direct involvement in the cult surrounding Anne Frank and it surprised me when he mentioned the 'many' people who had made use of Anne's story for their own profit. This was not the last time I would be surprised in this regard.

I didn't think it necessary for him to get involved officially as chairperson of the Fund and stir up a hornet's nest for himself. His letter gave me the courage to pursue this sordid affair on my own.

A couple of years later, Vincent Frank-Steiner resigned his position on the Fund's board of governors. Buddy Elias, Anne's nephew who lived in Basel, took over as chairperson.

II

I wanted to spare my children the kind of influence my mother had had on me over the years and the kind of demands my mother-in-law had made on Ruud and me. I knew I would have to give them their freedom, albeit by degrees. Raising teenagers in Amsterdam in the turbulent early 1970s was far from easy. Ruud had a demanding job and was often away on business, leaving me to shoulder most of the responsibility for the children. Our daughter soon discovered Amsterdam's café life and the freedoms that went with it and started to enjoy them to the full. But she and my two sons managed to pass their school finals without difficulty. If I felt it necessary at the time to steer my children in one or other direction, I knew I had to be particularly careful.

Both our sons turned out to be good sailors, but this didn't prevent the oldest from almost sinking during the Fastnet Race in 1985. The biennial international competition organised by the Royal Ocean Racing Club, in which participants were expected to sail around Fastnet Rock in the Irish Sea, was hit by a sudden storm that year and a number of people lost their lives. Damage forced several teams to abandon the race, including the team in which my son was taking part.

My entire family enjoyed sailing so much that I tried not to let them see how I had slowly but surely grown tired of being obliged to listen to three weeks of conversation about sea currents and wind directions. My interests lay elsewhere. But we bought a new boat – more comfortable than the old one – and after a couple of trips to England I suggested we should sail next time to Denmark. I knew it was one of Ruud's ambitions, and I didn't want him to be sorry for the rest of his life that he hadn't made the journey.

We encountered heavy seas on the way and I spent much of my time seasick in the rear cabin. I wasn't afraid. On the contrary, I had every confidence in the sailing abilities of my husband and sons.

As we approached the island of Funen, setting a course for Svendborg harbour, hundreds of swans formed giant blotches of white on the surface of the water surrounding us.

I called a Danish friend who lived on the other side of Funen. She suggested we sail round the island and put in at the harbour nearest to her home. 'No,' I said. 'We're hiring a car and we're driving.' I had had enough of the rigours of sea life for the time being.

Our daughter didn't join us on the trip and hadn't done for some time. She preferred to head off in the car with her boyfriend Rob. Both had decided to study medicine after they finished grammar school.

Our family doctor was also a fervent sailor. His boat was berthed in Muiden marina and we took trips together from time to time. He had been our doctor from the day we moved into our house on the Hunzestraat, during the first year of the German occupation. I was eleven then. I never spoke to him about it, but at a given moment he arranged for my sister, who came to the Netherlands twice a year to visit my mother, to look after our children together with my mother and allow Ruud and I to go to Italy.

Ruud's job as a buyer for a department store chain brought him to Italy four times a year. My sister grumbled at the idea of being left with the children, but she was no match for the doctor's powers of persuasion, or those of my mother for that matter. The children adored their aunt, especially our daughter, and that made up for a great deal.

Ruud's Italian assistant joined me for daytrips when we were there. Ruud spoke fluent Italian by this time and didn't really need her. We drove from Naples to Pompeii one day and visited Mount Vesuvius. Pompeii's paving stones interested me the most, worn flat by the carts that had ridden over them twenty centuries ago. There was a heavy mist that day and we didn't get to see the crater.

I also enjoyed Florence. I had read so much about the Renaissance over the years and now I had the opportunity to see it all in the flesh, as it were, including the frescos, Donatello's David, and Michelangelo's unfinished statues that had been intended for a papal monument.

I noticed during my visit to Florence that not everyone shared my enthusiasm about the place. We were invited for dinner to Antonio's house one evening. Antonio was one of the manufacturers Ruud worked with on a regular basis and he lived in an old palazzo on the River Arno. I was still bubbling over from the sights of the day and I talked with Antonio about it. Much to my surprise, our host, who spoke both French and English, informed me that he preferred modern art, in spite of the countless Renaissance treasures he had grown up with and had obviously seen. I looked around. Modern art on every wall.

I overheard Ruud talking to Antonio's wife about the bridge drives she organised in their house. She regularly invited him to join them when he was in Florence. I walked to the window and placed my empty whisky glass on the low sill. I made a habit of drinking whisky on such occasions.

It made me feel like one of the boys. I started smoking for the same reason, an addiction I indulged for no less than twenty-five years. I leaned against the window and looked out at the Arno below. In the distance to the left I could see the Ponte Vecchio with its little houses and their sloping roofs so typical of the region.

Antonio joined me at the window. He was probably scared I might fall out under the influence of the two glasses of whisky I had downed.

'I once heard an art historian say that ninety-eight per cent of all art is garbage,' I said, 'and much of it is made for commercial purposes, for sale over the counter.'

'You're right,' said Antonio, 'but it's important that we collect to avoid running the risk of losing something of real value.'

It was to take years before I came to share his opinion and gradually learned to appreciate and enjoy modern art.

The classes in art history I followed under Mrs s'Jacob had already opened a completely new world to me. Now I had the time to visit museums, especially the Stedelijk Museum in Amsterdam, which became a regular haunt, together with a group of lady friends. I also continued to take classes in literature at the Institut Français in Amsterdam after completing my Sorbonne exams.

One of my other pleasures was attending decorative crafts demonstrations, including stained-glass windowmaking and the art of the loom. Printing also interested me, and prompted me to take evening classes in the theory of etching at the local college of graphic art. Visits to a number of companies specialising in graphic design formed part of the programme.

I was still looking for something that could give some purpose to my life now that my children had grown up. In the middle of the 1970s, my interest in printing techniques and related crafts led me to sign up for a course in bookbinding being given in the studio of a graphic artist. The realisation of the exterior form of a book stimulated my curiosity. Bert Graafland, one of the few who still practised the art of bookbinding in those days, welcomed a small group of interested students into his studio. He himself had studied under Elisabeth Menalda, to all intents and purposes the only person in the Netherlands who had practised the profession in the 1960s, when bookbinding as an artistic craft had reached its lowest ebb. The absence of a reputable training programme in the Netherlands forced bibliophiles to take their precious books to France for binding. The craft was gradually revived in the Netherlands around the beginning of the 1970s, influenced by what was going on abroad together with a general increase in interest in crafts and handiwork at home. This was how I discovered bookbinding.

I enjoyed working with all the material involved in the process: paper, cardboard, linen, scissors and ruler. I learned all about the different kinds of glue that were used. The smell of gelatine-based glue was familiar to me. My father used to use the same golden syrupy substance to repair our antique furniture from time to time, and I could picture it gently simmering on a spirit stove.

Much later, when I was already a fully-qualified bookbinder, I discovered that my father had worked for a bookbinder in his early years. I had little doubt that my fascination for the craft and my decision to enrol for private lessons with Bert Graafland without the slightest hesitation were not coincidental. It was as clear as the light of day: I wanted to be an artistic bookbinder. It gave me the opportunity to combine my interest in literature, the exterior form of books and the decorative arts in one single activity.

Bert Graafland's sudden death two years later left me shocked and upset. But I had already decided to look for a new teacher before his death. I hadn't progressed beyond the technical aspects of the craft in those years and this wasn't enough for me. I wanted to go to Ascona in Switzerland and continue my studies at the Centro del bel Libro, but I didn't know how to break it to Bert Graafland. His death ultimately provided the solution, and I spent the following summer holidays in Ascona with Ruud and our son Job.

I got up before dawn for the half hour walk from the hotel to the atelier and made the return journey at six in the evening, tired but satisfied. Job and Ruud took walks in the magnificent surroundings and I had the most wonderful holiday I can remember. I was introduced to the many possibilities bookbinding had to offer and to all the different materials that could be used in the process. I returned to Amsterdam with two books, both furnished with a new binding, one in leather the other in parchment. The problem was that the director of the school, Hugo Peller, had been largely responsible for the finishing touches. I later learned that this was what he did with the work of all of his pupils.

Back in the Netherlands, I took additional classes in Wassenaar, where Mr Willems ruled the roost in his *Ambachtshuys* or House of Crafts. Willems's skills as a bookbinder were underestimated by his colleagues. He would regularly invite specialists from abroad to give demonstrations or classes and I often participated. His enthusiasm brought me inspiration.

I finally learned the tricks of the trade in Paris from Sün Evrard, a bookbinder with both professional expertise and enormous qualities as a teacher. Twice a year, during the vacations, she offered classes to groups of women of more or less my own age and with the same passion for bookbinding. Here we learned the finer details of artistic bookbinding, or *reliure d'art*, which enjoyed and continues to enjoy more respect in France than in the Netherlands, and its practitioners work at a higher level. I discovered that courses in picture framing were being offered at the same bookbinding school. Ruud seemed interested in the idea and I managed to persuade him to join me and to follow some classes.

After a number of years in training, I had finally mastered the art of bookbinding in all its facets. Ruud's picture framing course had come to an end by that time, but I felt completely at home with the group of French women who made up the class and had no problem continuing on my own.

I travelled near and far to attend every demonstration and exhibition that had anything to do with bookbinding or graphic design. We took the car to the Gutenberg Museum in Mainz on one occasion, and to the Plantijn Museum in Antwerp. During our travels, I even managed to persuade Ruud to visit the libraries of virtually every port of call and to take the time to look at their collections of antique books. He began to enjoy himself after a while, and my bookbinding acquaintances gradually became his.

In Venice, where Gutenberg's technique – printing with detached letters – had quickly caught on, I was now more interested in the incunabula in the library than the Renaissance works of Giorgione, Titian and Tintoretto.

I drove halfway across the Netherlands to attend a

demonstration on paper marbling, and halfway across Belgium to learn a paper decoration process from a bookbinder in Brussels who used sunlight as part of her technique. I also attended courses in Ghent.

From time to time I would restore a book and take the opportunity to acquire the material I needed to experiment with the techniques I had learned, such as a marble tray with Irish moss and paint for marbling and a screen for pressing handmade paper. But when I received an honourable mention for a binding I had submitted to a competition and sold the work to the Royal Library, I decided that my restoration days were over.

I started to make a name for myself as a designer bookbinder and commissions quickly followed. I bought my paper, leather and other materials in Paris and my atelier began to look more and more professional.

I wanted to know all there was to know and see all there was to see. I attended lectures on the aesthetics of book design given by Professor Gerrit Willem Ovink at the University of Amsterdam. Hendrik Vervliet, professor at the University of Antwerp, travelled to Amsterdam once a week to introduce us to the history of books. We learned all about ancient manuscripts from Dirk Obbink, who was later to become full professor at the University of Leiden where we were given the opportunity to see the real thing.

What makes a person want to dismantle a perfect machine-bound book and then go through the laborious process of rebinding it? It all seems a little pointless. But a book is not rebound because it needs a new cover. It serves as the inspiration for the creation of a work of art, and the technique of bookbinding is the means to that end. Bookbinding as an art form is not autonomous; it is always in service of the book being bound. Unlike ceramics or weaving, it cannot liberate itself from its primary function.

I wanted to create modern bindings that gave expression to the spirit of the age and that required knowledge of contemporary art movements in a variety of different domains. But before I could create my own designs, I had to throw everything I knew overboard as ballast. I didn't want to revert to the past or indiscriminately imitate.

My point of departure was that a book had to maintain its original book form no matter what, and that decoration should not extend beyond the cover. Nevertheless, in my own designs I looked for ways of transcending these dimensions. My first experiment in this regard was what I called 'moveable bindings'. I decorated a book on libraries by inserting spindles under the flat leather cover to create globes of the world. For a book on World War I, I added three cardboard rifles that could be folded outwards from the binding.

I also included boxes in the decoration process, thereby creating a spatial form together with the cover of the book. Other work exploited optical effects to make the cover appear to extend beyond its original dimensions. I had discovered the computer by this time, which allowed me to create a circle in which I placed the title in red leather. By adding perspective to the letters, I gave the circle spherical shape.

My bindings frequently won prizes and often became part of private and public – museums and libraries – book collections, both in the Netherlands and abroad.

From time to time I would work on a book object, an artwork that leaves the book form behind and gives free rein to the imagination. A gallery in Dusseldorf specialising in such objects discovered my work and invited me on a regular basis to take part in their commercial exhibitions.

The designer bookbinding world is a small one. As a result, the best-known binders from across the globe tend to know one another and like to keep in touch. They meet frequently at exhibitions where they often exhibit together or visit as a group. They also attend the same national and international symposia.

The quality of contact and communication between designer bookbinders at the international level can best be illustrated by an initiative taken by Swedish bookbinder Manne Dahlstedt, a man whose designs I admire for their craftsmanship, creativity and humour. Sixteen bookbinders from twelve different countries were given a work of art consisting of one or two folios and were invited to create an appropriate cover. In addition, they were asked to work in succession on a binding for a folio by the same artist; each added his or her contribution and sent the result on to the next binder. The project took almost two years to complete. When the results were finally exhibited in the Royal Mariemont Museum in Belgium, we all agreed to do something similar with the catalogue and have each of the contributing bookbinders work on it. The project was a success.

In 1994, I took part in an international bookbinding conference in Oxford entitled *New Horizons in Bookbinding*. But as fate would have it, I seemed to have less and less time available for the career I had intended to pursue for the rest of my life. I managed to submit a binding for the Tregaskis Centenary Collection at the very last minute and just in time to have it included in the catalogue. I had started work on it months before, but had kept putting off its completion. The collection was purchased by Manchester University Library. It was my last serious piece. These days I limit myself to simple book objects, boxes and other cardboard creations.

My painting activities had also ground to a halt and I had more or less abandoned the painting with the two towers. I had something else on my mind. I was planning to write a book.

III

A good forty years after Otto Frank and the original publisher of Anne's diary had asked me to write something about her on the occasion of the diary's first edition, I finally responded to their request. But this time I was writing for Anne, who could no longer write for herself. A sense of indignation inspired me to write, which I am certain Anne would have shared. Our friendship obliged me to put pen to paper.

I worked on the project for a full six months and then offered the manuscript to the publisher who had approached me after the appearance of the article in *Vrij Nederland*. He was satisfied with the text and started the editing process immediately, as I could see from the manuscript when he later returned it to me.

During our first conversation he told me he had also wanted to publish Eva Schloss's book, but had decided not to on the advice of Joke Kniesmeyer: 'I would steer clear of that book if I were you.' I asked him not to say anything to the Anne Frank Foundation about my book.

He had already edited a substantial part of the manuscript when he wrote a short letter to me telling me that the book, on closer inspection, hadn't lived up to his expectations.

I was disappointed, of course, but it wasn't to last. Willy Lindwer put me in touch with his own publisher, to whom he had recommended my manuscript. I sent him a copy before the weekend and received a response early the following week: 'Read it in one sitting … fascinating stuff.' The new publisher also agreed to say nothing to the Foundation about the book and not to consult the RIOD. Editing started anew and we signed a contract with a projected date of publication in October 1990.

When the book was ready to go to press, he contacted Joke Kniesmeyer about another book he was interested in publishing on the correspondence between the eighth person who had gone into hiding in the *Achterhuis* and his girlfriend Carlotta. It turned out that the Foundation had known for a while that I had been writing a book and that they were not planning to react to its publication. Joke Kniesmeyer gave him a copy of a letter addressed to the Foundation by Eva Schloss on the publication of the interview in *Vrij Nederland* in which she tried to challenge some of my claims. Her threat – 'If she doesn't put a stop to those insulting fabrications of hers, the consequences might be serious' – worried the publisher, who feared she might take legal measures, and he asked me to revise my book to avoid a possible libel claim. I did what he asked, although I was convinced of the truth of what I had to say. I enlisted the help of a lawyer to make the book even more reserved than it already was.

I presume that Eva's letter and threats had also been shown to the previous publisher and that he had buckled under.

Around that time, some friends invited us to a party. Franklin, our host – the one who had recommended I write my book – introduced me to another couple as the friend of Anne Frank and as the one who had bound a book he had in his possession. He fetched the volume, and since I rarely had the opportunity to talk about my work, I launched into an explanation. It was the book of poems about World War

I, the cover of which could be left open by resting it on three old fashioned rifles.

The conversation then moved on to Anne Frank and the couple appeared to be aware of my problems. I was still in a talkative mood.

The next day, I received a phone call from the woman with whom I had enjoyed such an animated conversation at the party. She asked me if I would agree to an interview on the topic we had been discussing. She worked for a national newspaper – *De Telegraaf*. I was delighted. Bookbinding rarely found its way into the papers, I said. But she wasn't really interested in bookbinding. She wanted an interview about Anne Frank that might serve as a sort of advance review of my book. Once again, I had forgotten the magical effects any mention of Anne Frank's name could have on a listener.

I told her I would think about it. I immediately called the publisher and told him it didn't appeal to me, but he welcomed the opportunity to publicise the book with open arms and I finally agreed to the interview.

'Have you any idea how many people read *De Telegraaf*?' Franklin asked, when I told him about my reservations. 'You would have to be mad not to do it. If only one per cent of the readers buy the book you'll be set up for life!' I never thought about numbers. His commercial approach made me laugh and I suspected that he had put me in touch with Henk van der Meyden's 'scout' on purpose, but I didn't pursue the matter.

Henk van der Meyden did the interview himself. I found him pleasant, and in spite of his disorganised appearance his questions were efficient and correctly followed up. I read his text prior to publication in order to verify its content. The article appeared with two eye-catching photographs.

It took a couple of days for the first reaction to appear in *De Telegraaf*, not from the Anne Frank Foundation this time, but from Eva Schloss herself in the form of a letter to the editor. The last sentence in particular caught my attention: 'It's difficult for me to prove that I knew Anne Frank.' What did that mean? Wasn't she allowed to wave Otto Frank's letters in the air as evidence anymore? Hadn't the Foundation used them in the past as proof that Eva and Anne had played together on the Merwedeplein?

My efforts were rewarded with a positive review of my book in *Vrij Nederland*. The reviewer's last sentence contained a clever paradox: 'We should be grateful to Eva Schloss for inspiring Jacqueline van Maarsen to write this book.'

I had jumped the gun a little when I told the Anne Frank Foundation that I was prepared to open an exhibition they had organised in Las Vegas. The question had come from Cor Suijk, but the invitation never materialised. Nevertheless, the organising committee invited me to visit a couple of weeks later and talk to some groups of schoolchildren about my friendship with Anne. 'They're looking forward to meeting you,' said Cor, who passed on their request. Ruud was also invited to accompany me.

I experienced what it meant in America to be 'Anne Frank's friend' when I visited Nevada. My own personality was completely concealed behind the celebrity I represented. When I talked about my friendship with Anne they were all ears. After a TV appearance and some photos in the newspapers, people started to recognise me on the street and talk to me. Teachers and children I visited at school hugged me, sometimes with tears in their eyes. An invitation to fly over the Grand Canyon in a private plane left me with mixed emotions, especially as I didn't have a good head for heights. We then moved on to Utah where the Mormons had invited us to give a talk. Here too our hosts treated us to a day out at one of Utah's National Parks.

Now that I had gone public, my memories started to confront me more and more. I had become a household name and people knew where to find me for interviews, films, documentaries and newspaper articles, without having first to consult the Anne Frank Foundation. Requests for interviews appeared from as far away as Japan, where Anne Frank was extremely popular. I didn't try to avoid them anymore, most of the time at least, partly because I had written a book and wanted to focus attention on it, and partly because I realised that I now had a contribution to make to the spread of the message Anne's diary contained.

In the years that followed I was able to combine these activities with my bookbinding work, but from the moment Cor Suijk asked if I would stand in for Miep Gies there was little time left for bookbinding.

Miep Gies had travelled the length and breadth of America for years giving lectures with Cor Suijk. The American author Alyson Gold had written a book about her and, after it was made into a film, Miep was worshipped in America as a hero.

One example of the respect she enjoyed was the honorary doctorate she had been invited to receive from Connecticut College in New London. She planned to attend the ceremony with Cor Suijk, but a couple of days before it was scheduled to take place she fell ill. Both Miep and Cor suggested that I, as a friend of Anne Frank, should receive the honorary doctorate in her name.

During the ceremony, I said a few words about Miep that I had put together on the plane. The applause was enthusiastic and lengthy, and the only way I could cope with the embarrassment was to return to my seat and put an end to it. The actress Mia Farrow, whose son was studying at the college, read an excerpt from Anne's diary. The college also organised a reading for the children the following day, to which they gave their undivided attention.

It became clear that Miep's health would not allow her to travel for a while, but engagements had been made. She was scheduled, for example, to be present in California at the screening of a documentary in which she herself featured.

Cor Suijk proposed to the host committee that two of Anne's friends should take Miep's place in California. As a result, Hannah and I were to meet once again, this time in Orange County. Hannah now lived in Jerusalem and we rarely saw each other.

A documentary by the English filmmaker Jon Blair was screened on the first evening, with live shots of Anne dating from 1940.

The fragment had an extraordinary history. The film shows Anne leaning out of the window and looking at a young married couple getting into a car in front of the porch of their house on the Merwedeplein. Decades later, the couple in question, Mr and Mrs Kalker, were looking at the 8mm film that had been made of their wedding. They had paid no attention to Anne's presence prior to that, but in the meantime Anne had become an international celebrity and they now recognised her as the girl leaning out of the window in the film. They contacted Otto Frank, showed him the fragment, and handed it over to him when they saw how much it had moved him. They are the only moving pictures of Anne in existence. They agreed at the time that he would never use the fragment for commercial gain, although he later made it available for a German documentary in 1979 celebrating what would have been Anne's fiftieth birthday. The Kalkers handed the entire film over to the Anne Frank Foundation after Otto's death and it was likewise agreed that it should not be exploited commercially. The Foundation granted Jon Blair permission to use the moving images of Anne in his documentary and it wasn't long before the fragment became a familiar sight the world over. I had attended the premiere of Blair's documentary in Amsterdam some weeks before, and had even appeared in it.

When I saw the fragment for the first time in a video of the 1979 German documentary, I was more focused on myself than anything else: my first television appearance, and in German no less! I never watched it again after that. But after seeing Anne in Jon Blair's film, I was entirely focused on her: my friend as she once was, a year before we became friends on the first day of the new school year, her hair cut short.

Jon Blair later gave me a copy of the video of his documentary, and when I watched it again I realised that Anne was not looking out of her own window in the fragment. Seen from the street, she was clearly in the neighbouring house, leaning to the left of the window frame and looking downwards to the right, precisely as she had done in the German documentary. I informed the Anne Frank Foundation immediately and added that Margot and her mother were watching from a window in the Frank family's apartment. The image of Anne's mother and sister was vague, but when I showed the video to my sister she recognised both women right away. The people responsible for making the film public hadn't noticed them – they were not familiar with either Margot or her mother. When the fragment was broadcast later in a documentary on Dutch television, which also featured an interview with the Kalkers, I realised that the subtitles had almost obliterated both women. I was asked to come to the Anne Frank House and explain what I had seen. Their reaction to my observation was aggravated and incredulous, especially to the fact that Anne was leaning from her neighbour's window. I heard nothing more from them about it.

It was also evident from the Dutch TV documentary that the Kalkers, who had given the fragment to the Foundation without asking a single cent in return, were enraged by the fact that it had now been used for commercial gain.

I have since seen the fragment of film with the moving images of Anne on more than a few TV documentaries. To my surprise I suddenly realised that Anne was leaning out of the right-hand corner of the window and must have been staring with interest at a well-known Amsterdam skyscraper instead of the recently married Kalkers on their way to their car. Could I have been so mistaken, I thought to myself, and I fetched the video of Blair's documentary just to be sure. I had not been mistaken. I could only conclude that the fragment had been turned around – not so difficult with 8mm film – to accommodate history! Anne was no longer leaning out of the neighbour's window, but the window of the Frank family's apartment, and so it was to be from then on.

Perhaps the commercialisation of the Anne Frank Foundation's activities was unavoidable. The controlled use of market forces might even have helped promote its goals, making a degree of vulgarisation tolerable to some extent. Perhaps the creation of Anne Frank the myth had been inevitable and relatively acceptable. But if all this forced people to bend the truth, then it was clear that the means had become more important than the end, more important than the ideals that the Foundation represented. As far as I was concerned, the film fragment was just one more example of truth bending.

But before rushing to offer my opinion on the matter, I decided to give it some further thought. Was it really such a terrible thing that the film had been turned around, and had it been done on purpose? And what if it had? What difference did it make if the film portrayed Anne looking out of her own window or that of her neighbours?

The only people who were genuinely interested in such issues were the Anne Frank historians, but I knew precisely why the matter upset me so much. It had to do with the unpleasant manner with which the Anne Frank Foundation had treated me – and on more than one occasion – when I drew their attention to something for historical reasons or because of the truth. My dissatisfaction with the repercussions that followed my likewise initially historical comments on Eva Schloss and her alleged friendship with Anne formed part of the same frustration.

But I had never asked myself 'what's the point?' and I never will. I have never been plagued by doubt, not even when I had to face an unwarranted storm of negative reactions. Every time I pictured my little friend Anne in my mind's eye and was reminded of her vivacity, her drive, her determination, I knew that resignation was not for me.

Hannah had made arrangements for the host committee in California to take us to Disneyland. Alyson Gold, who lived in Los Angeles and was writing a book about Hannah and her wartime experiences, had also invited her to visit Universal Studios and she asked me to accompany her. We were present the same evening at the screening of the documentary in which Miep Gies had featured.

A couple of years earlier, after finishing her book on Miep, Alyson paid me a visit and asked permission to write my story as well. She had once told me that she had romanticised Miep's story a little, arguing that it was a bit on the thin side for a full book. I had no plans in those days to write my own book, but I turned down her request nevertheless. The idea of a romanticised version of my own story did not appeal to me in the slightest. Hannah later told me that that was what she found so clever about Alyson's work: 'I give her a single sentence and she writes pages and pages,' she wrote in a letter.

Alyson sent me a copy of her book on Hannah when it first appeared in America. It turned out that her inclination to romanticise had inspired her to copy passages about my friendship with Anne from my book and include them in her own as if the events in question had happened to Hannah. She had apparently found Hannah's story about her friendship with Anne to be just as thin as Miep's, and although my own work had not yet appeared in America, I had given her a translation of the book that had been made by an American friend. I had absolutely no reason to suspect that she would use my story for her book about Hannah. She had promised to help promote the publication of my book in America, and that was why I gave her a copy of the translation.

Hannah herself was quite honest with me about the situation. She told me that she remembered little from the time, certainly when it came to our days at the Jewish Lyceum, where she spent more time with another girlfriend than with Anne.

I sent a letter of protest to Alyson, but received a noncommittal response. Hannah was equally flippant about the situation and did nothing to redress it. I decided not to bother her about it. A battle with Hannah on 'who was Anne Frank's *best* friend' was the last thing I wanted.

I agreed, as a result, to accept Hannah's invitation to attend the presentation of the Dutch translation of Alyson Gold's book about her in the new café of the Anne Frank House. Alyson was also present, but I made no further reference to the matter.

Both Hannah and I gave lectures in Orange County in Southern California. David Barnouw from the NIOD was also present, invited to provide some additional background to the documentaries. The turnout was poor, however, and the people seemed disappointed that Miep had not been able to attend in person.

I bumped into David Barnouw on a regular basis on the stairwell of our apartment in Amsterdam. His girlfriend lived in the same building complex. We would greet each other affably, but we never talked about my book, in spite of the fact that he must have read it by virtue of his job. He travelled frequently, giving lectures on Anne's diary.

Cor Suijk informed me that he had received a request from CNN for a live interview with both Hannah and myself. The preliminary interview was done by phone and the discussion was considered good enough to invite us to the CNN studios that afternoon. We imagined being welcomed into their unparalleled facilities – CNN wasn't the most famous and most watched TV station in the world for nothing – but we arrived into a dark little cubbyhole where we were just about able to distinguish the presence of two cameramen. The interviewer, who was nowhere to be seen, turned out to be in Atlanta, thousands of kilometres away, and we spoke to him via a TV monitor. He had a southern accent and we had trouble understanding him. We were able to follow the opening discussion, but when he turned to the documentary – we had only seen it the evening before and had not had the time to reflect on it – we were both at a complete loss. Hannah responded at one point to a totally incomprehensible question by turning to me and saying: 'You answer that question.' She put me on the spot, and while I was able to laugh about it later, I didn't find it funny at the time. I didn't think it appropriate to start bickering with her in front of half the American population and didn't want to be responsible for a long gap in the conversation. My response probably had little if anything to do with the question and the conversation petered out like a damp squib.

I never mentioned the incident in later conversations with Hannah, but I decided at that point to avoid appearances with her on television wherever I could. Where was the shy, sweet little girl I had once known? I started to long for home, for the peace and quiet of my atelier.

We travelled on to Houston, where the Holocaust Museum had requested our presence at the unveiling of a memorial plaque in honour of Miep and Jan Gies. The museum had been built by a number of American Jews from Houston, referred to in America as *survivors*, each of whom had his or her own wartime story to tell.

I had a conversation with one of them that evening at a party. He turned out to be one of the richest men in Texas. He had made his way to America from Poland with nothing more than the clothes on his back. He had survived the war in Poland because he didn't look Jewish and was able to get by working as a farmhand for a zealously anti-Semitic farmer. I could imagine that he had little interest in Anne's story, with such a personal wartime trauma to cope with.

Back in Amsterdam, my literary agent presented me with a letter from an American publisher: 'I would love to publish a book about Anne Frank, but not this book.' I can't prove it, but I have always had the feeling that opposing forces were at work trying to prevent the publication of my book by a regular publisher. As a result, I decided to publish it under my own steam as a supplement to my lectures.

My laboured relationship with the Anne Frank Foundation inspired them to avoid commenting on my book, or at least to distance themselves from it behind the screens. When such a powerful organisation takes such a stance, I presumed it must have been a signal to publishers to keep their hands off the book in question.

Miep, who was now well into her eighties, had recovered to some degree, but foreign travel was still too much for her. As a result, Cor Suijk would ask me on occasion to accompany him to America to give a lecture or two. He also organised appearances for Hannah. He would usually introduce the lecture himself and speak at length about his own story of war and resistance.

The extent to which the Americans were interested in my story inspired me. After a presentation I would answer questions from the floor and my sense of being part of the entire affair, something I had done my best to blot from my memory in previous years, grew by the day. I conquered my aversion to the discomforts of travel when I realised how important my relationship with Anne was when it came to drawing the attention of the children. Ruud accompanied me on most trips and that made things a great deal easier. Busloads of children were sometimes organised to come and listen to one of my talks. Standing in front of thousands of children is a daunting enough task, but to my surprise I had no difficulty with it.

A young American boy once asked: 'Why didn't you just take the plane and escape?' I realised then how difficult it was for children of today to understand what life was like in the Netherlands under German occupation. It was a life without freedom, detached from the outside world, in which transport possibilities were strictly limited if they existed at all. No trains, no boats, no cars, and in many places not even bicycles. The only planes we saw were high up in the sky, allied bombers on their way to bomb German targets.

I also gave talks for Jewish organisations, mostly during fundraising dinners at which I was top of the bill. People would regularly come over to me after such a meeting to tell me their own story. They were the survivors, like the man who had spoken to me in Houston. Often enough, people would tell me afterwards that they had never heard their friends or family members talk about their past. This was the first time for many of them. The survivors told me how they had lived through the war and its horrors and how they had finally found their way to America.

I met Eva Schloss once again in 1996, this time in New York during the presentation of The Spirit of Anne Frank Awards organised by the city's Anne Frank Centre. The prizes were awarded periodically to those who had made themselves useful on behalf of the cause. We had both been on the list of prominent individuals that constituted the Honorary Committee for years. Hannah was also listed. We had been invited to be present at the awards to add some lustre to the event, which took place at the Lincoln Centre. An American writer had put together a dialogue featuring Eva, Hannah and myself, and had sent it in advance for our approval. The idea was that each of us in turn would say something about our friendship with Anne using the author's words. I was outraged at first and refused to attend – Eva was scheduled to speak about her encounters with Anne that were now common knowledge across the globe – but after the organisers agreed on my request to change the lines to be spoken by Eva I decided to go through with it. Her story was to be restricted to her dealings with Otto Frank. The author was adamant that I be present and she was willing to move heaven and earth to have me there.

The meeting with Eva prior to the presentation was less than hearty. We said nothing to one another after the event. When we were later invited to speak to the press, I couldn't stop her from talking about her relationship with Anne and their childhood friendship.

Cor Suijk shot to prominence in 1998 when he revealed 'the five missing pages' from Anne's diary that had come into his possession. From that time onwards, he travelled regularly with Melissa Müllerto to promote her biography of Anne Frank. Melissa had been the first to hear the story of the missing pages and had included it in her biography. I knew Melissa well, and had met with her on numerous occasions in relation to her writing. I was reminded of the words of Franklin, our friend in Amsterdam, who had recommended that I write a book because a newspaper article wasn't weighty enough. The same could now be said for Cor Suijk, who had chosen the context of a book to publicise the five missing pages as well as announcing it in the papers.

The enormous popularity of Melissa's biography was due, in part at least, to those five missing pages, and the book was made into a mini-series for television. As a result, I was introduced to Ben Kingsley who was to play Otto Frank. He visited me at home in search of inspiration for his role. I met him a second time at the premiere in Washington. I still saw Ben Kingsley on the screen and not Otto Frank, but of all the actors who have approached the role, Kingsley comes closest to the real Otto.

Cor Suijk sold the five pages to the Dutch state, thereby completing NIOD's collection of Anne's writings. He used the money to establish an institute in America dedicated to instructing school teachers about the Holocaust. Hannah joined an organisation of famous speakers, which scheduled lectures on their behalf in America.

As the years passed, the target of my travels shifted and I spent more time speaking in Germany about Anne than America.

Travelling across Germany with my story of racism and discrimination was an extraordinary experience. Reactions differed considerably from those I had received in America. In Germany, the children and grandchildren of the perpetrators ultimately made up my audience. I adapted my lectures accordingly. The facts could not be denied, of course, but I stated my desire to understand the problem from the perspective of the post-war generation, those whose parents and teachers had often been Nazis and who were conscious of the atrocities committed by the older generation during the war.

I also encountered people in Germany who had their own wartime story to tell, inspired by my lecture. The headmaster of a German school, for example, opened up as he brought us back to our hotel. On the way from the hotel to the school, he had limited himself to organisational matters, but now, inspired by our visit, he told his own story. His father had kicked him out of the house when he was sixteen. His French teacher had spoken in class about German history after 1933, the year that Hitler came to power. In those days, history lessons in German stopped with that date. He had started asking his father critical questions, especially about his service in the Waffen-SS, but the man flew into a rage and refused to discuss the matter. His father remained an inveterate Nazi until the day he died.

At another school, a German girl stood up after my presentation. 'Anne Frank wasn't murdered by the Germans,' she said, 'she died of an illness.' I was taken aback and didn't know exactly how to respond for a moment. But the teacher who had organised our visit to the school and had prepared the students in advance understood the girl's remark. 'Who told you that,' he asked, looking at the girl searchingly, 'your parents?' 'My grandfather told me,' she replied shyly, 'when he heard that Anne Frank's best friend was coming to give a talk at our school.'

The teacher clearly found it difficult to contain his anger. 'Tell your grandfather that Anne did indeed die in Bergen-Belsen of typhoid, but that was because of the miserable conditions in the camp. The Nazis did not intend anyone to survive.'

There was also the occasional unpleasant encounter, the

absurdity of the associated story determining the extent to which it became planted in my memory. On one occasion I was invited to give a talk in a small town near Nuremberg. The man who collected me from the train pointed to a row of *Jugendstil* houses from the taxi. He was convinced that they had survived the allied bombs 'because they belonged to Jews who had managed to escape to America before the war'. An American pilot had told him about it in his local pub, he insisted. I asked in astonishment if the Jews in question had returned to claim their property after the war, but he had no answer. I knew in fact that nothing had survived of Jewish life in Nuremberg other than the Jewish cemetery. I was also familiar with the German word *Stammtisch* or 'pub regular' – and I answered: *Antisemitisches Stammtischgeschwätz* – 'anti-Semitic pub talk', hoping he would get the message.

I have never been able to understand why Anne Frank became so popular in Japan. Otto Frank had told me in the very early days that a church had been named after her and that a number of schools were destined to bear her name. Here too, young Japanese girls with adolescent problems and the resulting difficulties with their parents felt a bond with Anne, but that surely couldn't be the only reason for her popularity. I presumed it had something to do with Japan's own war record, with the horrors of Hiroshima and Nagasaki, which the Japanese associated with the terrible things that had happened to Anne Frank and her fellow Jews.

The fact remained, nevertheless, that when I sent my book to an agent in Tokyo, it only took a couple of months to produce a Japanese translation and I was invited to travel to Tokyo for the launch. It became clear from the correspondence that followed that the publisher not only wanted me to be there to promote my own book, but also to promote all the other books they had published on Anne, including *The Diary of Anne Frank*, the NIOD publication that had been translated unabridged into Japanese.

Nothing was too much for the friend of Anne Frank. Our hosts had asked me before my departure if I had any special wishes. I had responded in the negative. I had never had any desire to travel to the Far East and had no idea what to expect in the tourist department. But Ruud was keen to spend the night in a *ryokan* – a typically Japanese inn – and I asked if that could be arranged for him. Our Japanese hosts immediately booked us into the best *ryokan* in the country, situated in the most magnificent surroundings. I didn't really share Ruud's enthusiasm, especially when it came to sleeping on the floor.

The Japanese agent invited us to a French dinner at the American club of which he was a member. He picked us up in his Bentley, which wasn't out of place among the other luxurious cars parked in front of the club. The American Embassy Attaché arrived in a white Rolls Royce. Out of politeness, I drank more wine than I was used to that evening.

No trouble or expense was spared to draw the public's attention to Anne Frank and promote the sale of books related to her and her story. Schoolchildren were invited to take part in a competition with the possibility of winning a group trip to Amsterdam. I gave my talk at a number of schools, where the pupils listened in complete silence and asked questions afterwards in the most disciplined fashion.

The talk I was scheduled to give in Hiroshima presented me with a historical problem. How could I draw a connection between Anne Frank and the dreadful things that had happened there? I had read about a twelve-year-old girl by the name of Sadáko Susáki who had been struck down with leukaemia as a result of the atom bomb that had been dropped on the city. She was totally convinced that she would stay alive as long as she folded origami cranes. She folded 1,300 cranes and then she passed away. Just like Anne, I argued, Sadáko was one of the innocent children who had become the victim of war. I told my audience that the people in the far distant Netherlands had also heard about the dreadful events in Hiroshima, about the cloud that had mushroomed above the city after a fireball had lit up heaven and earth for a fraction of a second and destroyed countless lives in the process. We brought streamers with folded cranes to the children's monument. After the death of Sadáko Susáki, the streamers had become a symbol for the children who had died in the atrocity.

Everywhere I was invited to speak, crowds of people now waited in line to buy my book and have it autographed.

We made a return visit to Tokyo in 2000 on the occasion of an Anne Frank exhibition organised to celebrate four hundred years of international relations between Japan and the Netherlands. The idea was that I would bring some tangible memories of Anne with me for the exhibition, such as my poetry album in which Anne had written a verse, the first edition of *Het Achterhuis*, and the Monopoly game we had played together, which I still had in my possession.

Once again, I met Eva Schloss. She brought with her a cash ledger that Anne had filled with notes about the history of Greece and Egypt. The book had come into her possession after her mother's death and she was asked to make it available for the exhibition and bring it with her in person to Japan. As a result, the exhibition was opened by both of us, together with two Japanese gentlemen.

Even today, I hear regular reports from abroad that Eva Schloss is still doing the rounds with her story and that she even managed to have a stage play of her own book produced in which she meets a blanket-swathed Anne in the concentration camp, bending the truth to her own ends. Where had I heard that story before? It suddenly dawned on me that I had heard the two sisters who had been there when both Anne and Margot died talk about it on many an occasion. Anne had thrown away her lice-infested clothes and had spent the last days of her life wrapped in nothing more than a blanket.

But my anger has faded into resignation. I have done my duty, although the results I had hoped for remain unachieved.

My determination to keep my distance in the future from the Anne Frank Foundation didn't last, although I still managed to ignore everyone involved with the Foundation at the cremation of Jan Gies. The only person I spoke to was Joke Kniesmeyer, who came over to me and greeted me warmly.

I was regularly invited to events that took place in the Anne Frank House as if everything in the garden was lovely. After all, I was one of a very small few who had known Anne well. I was part of the legend. Initially, I ignored the invitations, including one to come and view the rooms in the *Achterhuis* that had been furnished in preparation for a film. I was curious to see what they looked like, but I didn't want to meet anyone and decided to visit at another time.

But after a while I started to take up the invitations again. I had resigned myself to the fact that my attempt to expose Eva Schloss had failed. I put the failure down to the Foundation's refusal to support me in my efforts, but was comforted by the realisation that I had maintained my integrity and had continued to back my friend Anne in spite of the opposition. In addition, I still had a connection with the ideals of the Anne Frank Foundation, in which Anne was ultimately pivotal. But when I got into a conversation with one of the associates at the Anne Frank House about the Eva Schloss affair I encountered a wall of silence.

A celebration was organised in 1999 in the presence of Queen Beatrix and Prince Claus on the opening of a new exhibition centre, an annexe to the house on the Prinsengracht, at which President von Weizsäcker of the German Federal Republic was to give a speech. Eva Schloss was also there with her husband and we gave each other the cold shoulder as usual during the customary VIP reception that followed.

As we stood in line to be presented to the Queen, Prince Claus came over to me and told me what he had felt at visiting the exhibition in the museum's recently renewed annexe.

The German president also had a chat with me. I felt obliged to give some content to our discussion so I told him about my lectures in Germany and about the fact that I had recently been inspired to adapt my usual talk during a visit to Brandenburg. I had introduced a story about Elector Friedrich Wilhelm von Brandenburg who had studied in Leiden for a number of years in the seventeenth century and had later married Louise Henrietta, the daughter of William of Orange. Connections with the Netherlands had had an enormous influence on Brandenburg's attitude to nonconformists such as the Huguenots and the Jews. Freedom and tolerance towards the Jews were just as wide-ranging in Brandenburg at that time as they were in the Netherlands. He listened politely to what I had to say, but I realised from a passing remark that the story was already familiar to him. Showing off one's knowledge in front of a historian can be a dangerous thing, even if he is a president.

IV

People's capacity to appropriate Anne Frank for themselves became painfully clear to me in the case of Rosa, the woman who used to visit my parents before the war and who had been friendly with Ruud's mother. I had visited her every week for years on end.

My preoccupation with the entire affair was such that at a given moment during one of my weekly visits I shared my discovery that Eva Schloss had made unfounded claims about her relationship with Anne Frank. I also told her about the Anne Frank Foundation and read her the letter I had sent to the board of governors. She listened, but had little to say in response and didn't offer any advice when I asked for it. She said yes to everything, which wasn't her custom, and she dismissed the letter I read to her with a couple of critical, off the point remarks. I was surprised at her reaction and felt a little ill at ease. I had no idea what to think about it.

The solution to the puzzle presented itself a couple of weeks later. A niece of her deceased husband Max was on a visit from Israel with her twelve-year-old daughter. 'And then the child asked me,' she related, "Rosa, don't you think I look like Anne Frank?" She knew that I had known her. I said, "Yes, from the side you do look like her."' And she went on to say that the ice between her and the otherwise difficult girl had been broken and that she had asked her all sorts of questions about Anne.

I was astonished and speechless. But when I stopped by

the following week I told her that although it wasn't pleasant for me to raise the matter, both she and I knew that she had never met Anne Frank in her life. I also told her that the stories she told about Anne to impress others were her own business, but that she had better keep them to herself as far as I was concerned if she didn't want to disturb our relationship of trust. She looked me straight in the face and said: 'Let's not talk about it anymore.'

It wasn't in her nature to admit to weakness and I took her response to be an avoidance of the truth. I continued my weekly visits, but I couldn't help feeling that our relationship had been seriously dented. I no longer looked forward to seeing her and regularly skipped a week. And I no longer spoke to her about the things that consumed my life in those days.

I kept this up for a year, but the situation changed after Ruud joined me on one occasion. Now that he was present she started to talk about Anne Frank again, probably hoping to gauge Ruud's thoughts on the matter. Ruud, who was familiar with Rosa's previous history, and had been updated by me on the latest developments, had already dismissed the entire story as ridiculous. We were hoping that Rosa would admit that she had invented what she had said, but she refused point blank. She had even managed to fantasise a few extras in the year that had passed.

I had reached the end of my tether and I wrote her a letter telling her I could no longer bring myself to visit her.

The entire affair went from bad to worse. She tried to renew contact with us, but refused anything resembling a candid admission that she had invented her relationship with Anne. Her most drastic concession was to admit that 'people remember things in their own way'.

We later heard from someone who knew Rosa from their French conversation group that she had talked about me and said that I was 'a little confused'.

Our relationship with Rosa was never to recover. She died a couple of years ago.

V

Much to our relief, my mother never returned to the subject of Jeanne and the inheritance. It had preoccupied her intensely and marred a large part of her life, but now it appeared to have been wiped from her memory.

But for Ruud and myself there were still a number of loose ends to be dealt with. We received a steep bill from the dealer employed to empty Jeanne's house. He hadn't been able to find much to his liking in the place and had had a lot of work emptying it. We hoped to be able to recover his costs from the notary together with the expenses I had incurred when I travelled to France. It was obvious to us that he had lured me to the village under false pretences. We had missed out on the inheritance, but the beneficiaries had gained from my presence and we felt we shouldn't be out of pocket.

I wrote a letter to the notary. Although I expected nothing from him, I inquired nevertheless after Jeanne's handbag and told him what I thought about its disappearance in no uncertain terms, including the fact that I had a witness who could confirm that Jeanne had taken the handbag with her when she moved in with her sister. I also told him about Jeanne's three wishes. She and my uncle had intended to leave their property to their nieces and not to her ninety-seven-year-old sister, or to a nephew no one had ever heard of, as the notary must have observed. She had also wanted to be buried wearing her earrings, but we had been unable to confirm the fact because everything had been taken care of without consulting us. I concluded by informing him that my aunt had wanted to be buried next to her husband in the village in which they had been so happy together. I added that friends of the family living in the village were aware that this was her last wish and insisted that he make the necessary enquiries about it.

I included a copy of the bill for emptying the house and summed up my expenses, asking him to transfer the amount to our account. He was responsible, after all, for settling matters related to the inheritance.

No answer was forthcoming. After six weeks had passed, I asked a notary – a friend of my son – if he would draw his colleague's attention to my letter, hoping it might make some impression. His answer arrived in the mail a week later. He informed me that he had nothing to do with us, only the beneficiaries. He was not a private detective, nor was he a magistrate. As far as the costs we had incurred were concerned, he would have to consult the beneficiaries for their permission. A postscript informed me in passing that the handbag had been found at the neighbour's house. Apart from a couple of letters, a bank book and a bunch of keys, the handbag had been empty. There was no sign of the codicil or the banknotes. He had apparently been unperturbed by the fact that the neighbour had made no mention of the handbag for so many months and not volunteered it, especially since he himself had no keys at his disposal to get into the village house and had been obliged to ask me to bring them with me.

I sent the notary a second copy of the bill a couple of weeks later when we realised that the money had not been transferred into our account. He didn't respond to it and I decided not to pursue the matter any further. I had no intention of allowing the inheritance to ruin my life, as it had my mother's to some degree. I simply didn't want to think about it anymore.

As a result, I lost interest in travelling to France. I had had enough for the time being of everything the entire sordid affair would undoubtedly remind me of. I stored the plastic bag with the photos and letters I had retrieved from the house in the cellar and left it undisturbed. I gave my sister the photo I had found of her together with uncle Albert's *Croix de Guerre*. My youngest son expressed an interest in Jeanne's clock. The birds were later to spread their wings on his mantelpiece.

I removed the painting with the two towers from the easel and set it against the wall, its back facing outwards. It was almost finished, but the towers themselves still needed some work. I didn't want to be reminded every day of the Eiffel Tower, and thoughts of the Westertoren next to the Anne Frank House now left a bitter aftertaste.

A year after Jeanne's death, my mother celebrated her hundredth birthday, complete with a floral tribute from the local authority and a telegram from the queen's secretariat. We opened her birthday post on her behalf and showed her the letter.

'From the Queen,' I said.

'Ah, *la reine*, the Queen,' she replied. She took the letter, folded it, and popped it into her blouse.

We had told her that morning that she had reached the ripe old age of a hundred, and in spite of the fact that she had never wanted to celebrate her birthdays, she now looked like a princess surrounded by the flowers, and behaved as if reaching a hundred was the most natural thing in the world, graciously receiving everyone's congratulations.

The various stages of geriatric dementia accelerated from

then on. As time passed, her memory gradually restricted itself to the period around the beginning of her marriage where it finally settled. She had no recollection of events after that.

Her three grandchildren took turns to visit her. She was happy to see them, but had no idea who these young people were who frequently spoke French to her and held her hand. Moments after they had gone, she could no longer remember their visit.

I still found it difficult to accept that my mother's always brilliant mind was decaying. When she started to talk about my father in the present tense, I said: 'But maman, papa has been dead for almost forty years.' And when she asked once why she saw so little of her parents, I helped her to work out how old she actually was and she then realised that it would have been impossible for her parents to still be alive. '*Je perds la tête* – I'm losing my mind,' she said.

I then noticed that it saddened her and left her feeling uneasy. From that moment onwards I shared in her conversations. She once said to Ruud: 'You should come to our place in the village. I'll ask my mother to make one of her delicious French meals for you.' She had no idea she was speaking to my husband. They always spoke French together, and it was clear she had mistaken him for my father. When he told her they should set a date, she nodded approvingly and then floated back with a smile to the past that had now become her present.

After the dealer had emptied the house through Alain's mediation, I returned to the village with Ruud and my sister. As we approached the house we noticed that the shutters – the ones that were still hanging – were wide open, creaking and clattering in the wind. Chantal had told us in a letter that squatters had set up camp in the house, breaking in through a cellar window. When they finally left, Alain boarded up the forced window with a plank of wood.

We went inside. The walls of the rooms had been daubed with fascist and obscene slogans and drawings and there were filthy rags lying all over the place. A fire had also been started on the living room floor and we were told that the place had almost gone up in flames. I was suddenly overcome by an intense feeling of pity for my mother. She had bought this house in 1923 with immense joy, not for herself, but for her parents and for her ungrateful brother who had profited from it longer than anyone else. But I dismissed these sentimental thoughts, comforted by the awareness that she would never have to witness this dreadful neglect and would remain blissfully ignorant of the damage that had been done to her property. In the deep recesses of her mind, this house still existed in all its former glory. She could go there whenever she wanted and her mother would tell her all the latest village gossip.

We had come to the village to hand over the sale of the house to an agent. It was to take several years before he managed to sell what had turned into a ruin. He wasn't able to raise much more than the value of the land.

The property was sold to a young couple who wanted to restore it themselves. Every now and then, if we're on a trip to Paris, I convince Ruud to agree to a detour and we drive through the village unobserved. Much to my satisfaction, the house has slowly returned to its original glory.

A couple of weeks after returning from the village and organising the sale of the house, my mother's condition started to deteriorate. We drove to the home immediately and met my sister in the corridor outside her room: 'It's not good,' she said, 'she's running a fever.'

We went inside and I walked over to the bed. Her hands fumbled restlessly over the bedclothes and she coughed incessantly. She didn't recognise me. The thought of her dying was farthest from my mind and I asked the doctor what he was planning to do.

'We've given her the necessary medication, but it doesn't seem to have made much of a difference.'

'But surely there's something else you can do,' I resisted.

'Should I take her to hospital?' asked Job, who had noticed my desperation. Job had finished his studies by that time and was specialising in clinical geriatrics.

'At your mother's age, I would consider it ethically irresponsible to try to prolong her life with patch and mend procedures,' said the doctor sternly.

My mother calmed down after a while.

'You should go home,' the nurse recommended. 'I'll call you if there are any changes.'

When we returned the following morning, the fever had subsided and the cough was less pronounced. She was much more lucid than the day before and recognised me immediately when I sat beside her on the bed. We were on our way to a memorial service for our daughter's mother-in-law who had been run over by a car in front of her house a couple of days earlier and had died from her injuries. We weren't sure if we should stay or leave.

The nurse arrived, fluffed up my mother's pillows and left again.

My mother glared at me, all at once. '*L'infirmière*, the nurse,' she spluttered. I stood up to call the nurse.

'No, no,' said my mother, 'the nurse, Jeanne's handbag, what did they say?'

I was at my wits' end and turned to Ruud. I had no idea what to say, but Ruud suddenly had an idea.

'Didn't you hear,' he said to his mother-in-law. 'They arrested the nurse. When Jeanne told her she wanted to return to the village, the nurse gave her the wrong pills. After Jeanne died, she stole the codicil from her handbag and gave the bag to Jeanne's neighbour with her bank book and a couple of unimportant letters. She's now in prison.'

'Ah, ça c'est bien, that's good to hear,' said my mother and she said nothing more about it. An expression of satisfaction appeared on her face and she fell into a restful sleep.

We asked the doctor if we should stay or go to the memorial service in Oosterbeek. 'It's hard to say,' he said, 'but it looks as if she's out of danger for the time being.' We decided to go to the service and pop in again on the way back.

The service in the small, centuries' old church took an eternity. British military khaki was everywhere. They had travelled from England in large numbers to pay their final respects to the woman who had been a beacon to them in the darkness of the war. The allies landed in the Netherlands in September 1944, far behind enemy lines, with orders to blow up five bridges and thereby put an end to hostilities. It turned out to be a bridge too far, as it were, and the dream of bringing the war to a speedy end quickly passed. The allied airborne landing troops were forced to retreat with considerable loss of life and injury to the outskirts of Oosterbeek.

Our son-in-law's parental home – he was yet to be born at the time – welcomed the wounded. Rooms were cleared to make space for stretchers carrying the injured and the dying. More and more soldiers were brought in, and the improvised infirmary had to be enlarged continually. They even had to use the space under the stairs. There was no running water, only a pump in the garden. There weren't enough provisions for the three hundred or more wounded soldiers, and medicines were also in short supply. Kate's beautiful linen was shredded to make bandages and they finally succeeded in helping those they could. Kate nursed the wounded and had a smile and a word of encouragement for all of them. Her husband was not at home because of the war and she had to look after her five children on top of everything. She brought them to the cellar, where they spent the night in sleeping bags on the floor. The soldiers who survived called her the Angel of Arnhem, and clearly never forgot her.

When the service was over, we called my sister and asked how the patient was bearing up. 'I would hurry if I were you,' she said.

She and her husband were waiting for us. A gesture of dismay was enough. My mother had died half an hour earlier.

Job played an elegy for cello by Fauré at the funeral and I read a passage from the book I had written two years earlier: words about my mother, about the courage and determination that had saved our lives during the war, the life of my sister and myself, and the life of my father.

VI

I caressed my ancient Krause paper cutter one last time before they took the one-hundred-and-fifty-year-old Heidelberg machine away. I had bought it with my first earnings and it had enjoyed pride of place in my atelier for twenty-five years, but there was no room for the colossus in our new house. My bookbinding activities had ground to a halt at the time, and there was room on my bench for a smaller electric cutter if I needed one.

The removal men wanted to finish their work the following day, and most of our possessions had been packed into boxes and filled the rooms downstairs. But I still had to make a start on my atelier. We had rushed off to France where a friend had just bought a house and had asked us to go with her to the notary's office. She didn't like the idea of having to face a French notary all on her own. I understood her reservations. My own experience of the world of French notaries was already several years behind me, and although my sister could still get wound up about the material side of the affair, it was only the discrimination that had left its mark on me, the notary and his companions' latent anti-Semitism. I had made my peace with it by then, but it had still contributed to my decision to continue giving talks about discrimination and racism, and about Anne's diary, which demonstrated what can happen when prejudice is driven to the extreme.

I started to clear up my atelier and by the end of the morning it was empty and the removal boxes were packed.

All that remained were the enormous sheets of cardboard against the wall. I tied them up with a length of rope and manoeuvred them against the pile of boxes.

It turned up behind the cardboard, the unfinished painting of the two towers: the Westertoren and the Eiffel Tower. It had been facing the wall for years and I had paid no attention to it. So much had happened in my life in the intervening years that it had slipped my mind completely.

It wasn't a bad painting, I thought, examining it carefully. I rummaged around in one of the boxes for my paint, completed the two towers in the midst of the removal chaos, and stood back to look at the result. Not perfect, far from it, but my heart and my soul had gone into it and were still present.

I headed for the door with the painting. The paint would still be wet the following day and it would have to be carried by hand. I took a final look around my atelier. I was determined to remember every last detail.

Author's note

The photographs of Otto and Anne Frank used on the cover and the photograph of Otto Frank, 1978, are the property of the Anne Frank Foundation. The photographs of Prinsengracht 263, and of the Westertoren from the Prinsengracht, 1954, are the property of the Maria Austria Institute. The remainder of the photographs used in the present volume are the private property of Jacqueline van Maarsen.

The photographs on the cover (from top to bottom): Anne Frank, Jacqueline van Maarsen, Eline (Jacqueline's mother) and Otto Frank.